Potent Fictions

Many of the narratives with which children are powerfully engaged are now designed by the toy and media industry and are delivered by television, computer games, comics and pulp fiction. Teachers are worried that these are affecting the standards and quality of literacy within schools. Furthermore, there is concern about the effects on children's growing consciousness of highly stereotyped, gendered narratives.

Based on close empirical work with children and a knowledge of cultural theory, this book describes and discusses the current market for children's popular culture, and the implications this has for classroom practice. It shows how children use many literacies and experiences to make sense of the world around them. It also argues that popular culture can take a place alongside more crafted literature as a vital resource of learning.

This book will help teachers to understand and engage with children's literacy practices outside school, whilst at the same time developing more traditional school practices of reading and writing. By developing an integrated approach to different narratives, teachers will enable children to develop literacy in its widest and most empowering sense.

Mary Hilton is currently Senior Lecturer in Primary Language and Literature at Homerton College, Cambridge. She is also an experienced primary school teacher.

Potent Fictions

Children's literacy and the challenge of popular culture

Edited by Mary Hilton

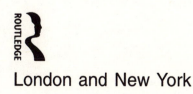

London and New York

First published 1996
by Routledge
11 New Fetter Lane, London EC4P 4EE

Simultaneously published in the USA and Canada
by Routledge
29 West 35th Street, New York, NY 10001

Selection and editorial matter © 1996 Mary Hilton,
individual chapters © their contributors

Phototypeset in Palatino by Intype London Ltd

Printed and bound in Great Britain by
TJ Press (Padstow) Ltd, Padstow, Cornwall.

British Library Cataloguing in Publication Data
A catalogue record for this book is available from the British Library

Library of Congress Cataloguing in Publication Data
Potent fictions : children's literacy and the challenge of popular
 culture / edited by Mary Hilton.
     p.   cm.
  Includes bibliographical references and index.
   1. Language arts (Elementary)   2. Literacy.   3. Popular culture.
 4. Mass media and children.   5. Mass media in education.
 I. Hilton, Mary.
 LB1576.P677   1996
 372.6044—dc20   95–25983
                                                                    CIP

ISBN 0–415–13530–3

This book is dedicated to all the children and teachers who helped us in this project. Without their time, patience, insights and wit it would never have been written.

Contents

Contributors

The idea for the book is reflected in its construction: that is, it has grown out of a number of conversations and concerns expressed by several teachers, students and lecturers at Homerton College, Cambridge about the growing 'threat' of the vast amount of popular culture aimed at children in Britain and the effects of this on literacy work in schools. Both the in-service Advanced Diploma course on language and literature and the third-year tripos course for undergraduates, 'changing literacies', involve the students in empirical work on children's literacy practices in and out of school, and on both courses evidence is continually gathered showing the power and pervasiveness of current media narratives, toy adverts, comics, artefacts and young teen magazines and cultures. The authors are therefore linked as a team, as we have already shared evidence, concern, theory and development. Although each contributor brings his or her own work and insights to their particular chapter the book has a shared theoretical base and a shared commitment to an empowering model of literacy teaching and learning.

Helen Bromley is currently Deputy Headteacher of Sunnymede Infants School in Billericay. She works part-time as a member of the Homerton Primary Language Team and has contributed to a wide variety of in-service courses for teachers. She has published several articles and chapters on the development of literacy in the early years and has worked with the BBC on *Teaching Today*. She has recently been involved in the preparation of a documentary film for the BBC on the teaching of reading.

Mary Hilton is Senior Lecturer in Primary Language and Literature at Homerton College, Cambridge. She teaches on both undergraduate and postgraduate courses, specializing in socio-linguistics, children's literature and the development of children's writing. She has been a deputy headteacher in a county primary school and holds an MA in education and an M.Sc. in social and educational research. Her main study is in community literacy practices. She has published chapters on the development of children's historical thinking, on popular culture and vernacular literacy. She has worked on media studies projects funded by the BFI and The Open University and has written for and advised BBC children's educational television.

Cathy Pompe has worked as a primary teacher, lecturer and advisory teacher on media education for Cambridgeshire and as research and planning officer for schools television, particularly consultancy work for the BBC series *Watch* and *Zig Zag*. She has set up classroom work featured on the programmes and has gathered ideas and written programme notes. She has carried out production work and created the Cambridge Media Education Resource Base. She has published numerous articles, chapters and reviews on media education, children's literacy and the toy industry. She has also written for The Open University, *Times Educational Supplement* and Cambridgeshire LEA and has carried out a BFI-funded research project on primary media education.

Isobel Urquhart is Senior Lecturer in Education at Homerton College, Cambridge. She also teaches and lectures at Anglia Polytechnic University. She has worked in secondary schools as a special needs teacher of literacy and has carried out research in this area for Essex LEA. She hold an MA in education from Aberdeen University and an MA in education research from Anglia Polytechnic University. She has written and published on teaching and learning strategies, and on boys' and girls' stories and psychotherapeutic dialogues.

Gill Venn is Senior Lecturer in the Department of Education at Anglia Polytechnic University. She teaches initial teacher training courses and in-service courses with students who are studying for higher degrees. Her major specialisms are equality and pastoral issues. She holds an M.Ed. in research into active learning methods in pastoral work. She has been head of faculty in an inner London comprehensive and is currently researching the problems of black student teachers in predominantly white schools. She has published on gender issues and pastoral care.

David Whitley is Senior Lecturer in English at Homerton College, Cambridge, where he teaches literature and media education. He has taught media studies in further education colleges. He has worked for a number of years in a special school for emotionally disturbed adolescents. His research interests include aspects of writing and culture from the Middle Ages to the eighteenth century. He is particularly concerned with the development of the fable as a form of children's literature and has published in this field. He is also interested in the use of narrative in the primary classroom.

The children of this world

Mary Hilton

For the children of this world are in their generation wiser than the children of light.

(Luke 16: 8)

It is commonly understood that books on culture address themselves to areas of our lives where we have a limited understanding, where there are gaps and silences. This book, on the other hand, attempts to involve itself collaboratively and passionately in ongoing *talk*. It has grown out of many discussions, arguments and conversations, in classrooms and staffrooms, round coffee trolleys, breakfast and dinner tables, photocopiers and bars. It hopes to contribute to and further that vital talk, to explore some of the current concerns about children and their exposure to today's flood tide of popular culture: videos, toys and comics, advertisements, computer games and magazines. It is not a book of answers, or even clearly defined questions, rather one which, we hope, is rich with further discursive points and possibilities. It attempts to make a sensitive contribution to the arguments about the stereotypes of gender and race to which children are exposed. It addresses itself to the web of concerns which include anxieties about the threatened nature of childhood itself and the role that media stories, particularly videos, play in our culture. It concerns itself, too, with the various ways in which literacy practices, literature in school and the demands of the National Curriculum affect the work of teachers.

The lived realities of their work, the cultural and social issues teachers confront on a daily basis and their theories of method are often ignored by social commentators and political interests. Curriculum documents which have been produced from outside the profession barely acknowledge the sophisticated media literacy of the young. Yet teachers know that in their classes many children are deeply engaged with reading and receiving pleasurable narratives from a vast and lucrative culture industry for children: imaginations captured by warrior figures, Barbie dolls and the latest Disney film. This cultural fact inevitably affects the literature the children prefer, the stories they write, the images and vocabulary they use quite naturally. More importantly, it powerfully affects their developing subjectivities, their concerns, their forms of self expression, their relationships and their world-views.

So this book attempts to speak to the heartlands of concern in the schools themselves and make its, albeit written, contribution to the discussion. It attempts to go straight to the matter of the school English curriculum in the primary and early secondary school classroom and there locate its critical discourse about children and popular culture. Through discussion of theoretical and social issues and work with real children its aim is to argue once again that teachers and children need time and space to tackle a variety of texts, to understand how they are constructed, to build a creative culture of mediation, imagination, transformation and resistance in the classroom.

Looking at the many ways literacy can be presented, our starting-point is that children are not passive readers, they actively engage with texts in the same way they engage with life. But, more than ever when confronted with such seemingly desirable stories and products outside school, they need discursive space, sympathy and imaginative and moral challenges inside the classroom in order for them to integrate what they watch, hear and read. In particular, they need to engage with literacy practices which empower them to unlock further texts, to experience various subject positions and diverse philosophies, to help them grow as citizens with a sense of imaginative possibility, power, responsibility and hope. In presenting these affective spaces, literacy practices and challenges, teachers need to have renewed confidence in a highly responsive theory of method, a belief in an educative process which allows them to listen to and to value the many readings, texts and literacies which help construct different children's growing consciousnesses in and out of school. This book hopes to contribute to the recognition and reinstatement of the overriding importance of that responsive educative process.

THE MYTHS AND REALITIES OF LITERACY LEARNING

With the advent of compulsory schooling in the late nineteenth century, but possibly before then, an idea, a working image of the effective young literacy learner became fixed in many people's minds – an image which social, linguistic, psychological and educational research has since proven to be erroneous. Yet it has become the common cultural property, the dangerous *common sense* of the nation. That idea is of a young child arriving in school as a blank sheet, a *tabula rasa*, an empty vessel. The clear duty of the teacher is then to show this completely ignorant child how to read and write starting, as it were, from scratch. Because this child has no previous knowledge and brings only a range of wilful emotions which need to be schooled into submission for proper learning to take place, literacy teaching consists in presenting this child with a series of graded, decontextualized exercises in reading and writing skills, which gradually increase in difficulty and complexity, under conditions of surveillance and control. Motivating these children, through promises of rewards or punishments, to carry out graded tasks, fitting the level of difficulty to the perceived ability of each child and generally creating and maintaining a calm and disciplined environment is, then, the accepted professional competence on which the teacher can be judged. In addition, the literacy practices of school are assumed to distribute evenly, through generalized instruction, a neutral technology, a handy toolkit which can be used effectively to unlock any text in the same way to result in the same schooled understanding.

Even in the elementary schools 100 years ago this model was proving to be unsatisfactory. Literacy teaching handed out as a graded body of set skills completely failed to allow children to make connections between different bodies of knowledge; the written symbols of school literacy on one hand and the detailed knowledge of the world of experience and home on the other. A huge number of children, well over half the school population, left school with the minimal skills which allowed them to decode the most simple text and only able to *copy* in writing. The system of 'Standards', where different levels of skill were rigidly defined and tested, was also an impediment to *applying* the skills required to anything other than the stated, somewhat meaningless passages from primers and readers, with the result that many pupils gladly gave up bothering with reading or writing when the required Standard was reached. According to David Vincent in his book *Literacy and Popular Culture: England 1750–1914*, the inspectors' continuing dissatisfaction with this state of affairs was focused on the assertion that the schools were failing to develop the 'intelligence' of their pupils. He quotes the school inspector for Finsbury in 1881, defining the problem with reading:

> This failure in intelligence does not, I am convinced, arise from want of previous hard work on the part of the teacher – on the contrary hard work is often too painfully evident – but rather from the want of *a more intelligent system of training the children to observe and think for themselves.*[1]

As Vincent points out, the old assumption that children were entirely ignorant was gradually being replaced by a realization that they were not being equipped with the means of enlarging and transmitting the knowledge they already possessed. The formal, structured, graded introduction to literacy skills was systematically denying many children the opportunities to make literate sense of their experience and, therefore, to write for themselves or to connect their lives with literature. The literacy practices they were learning were thus demeaning and dysfunctional in terms of individual intellectual or political growth. The schools supplied a generation of clerks with copperplate handwriting, sufficient to maintain the business of a growing empire, but rarely were these skills put to personal use or for organized resistance to controlling authority.

> Their grasp of the tools of written communication was so mechanical that only the very gifted or those who could establish an organized context within which to sharpen and apply their reading and writing skills stood any chance of resisting the fissiparous pressures of middle-class professionals, politicians, employers and entrepreneurs.[2]

Again and again since the nineteenth century educated professionals who work with children and language have pointed out that this graded and mechanical model of literacy teaching is ineffectual, inappropriate in an advanced industrial nation, expensive in time and money and is based on an intellectual misconception of how learning actually takes place. The fact that this model of literacy learning is also dangerously authoritarian, disguising a 'naturalizing' force where the literacy practices and literature of a small elite are the only ones taught, a culturally restricting approach in a democratic nation, is also mentioned, earning its critics a reputation for 'left-wing' inefficiency. English teachers have thus suffered continuous berating from a mistaken and often malicious press,[3] a series of political statements about the inadequacies of English teaching from Conservative politicians and a stream of new graded exercises and skills-based workbooks continuously marketed by enterprising publishers. And yet, across the nation, teachers are working successfully with another model, one based on a far more sophisticated and well-documented understanding of the child learner and a far greater appreciation of the active role of texts, particularly literary ones, in our cultural lives.

THE LEARNING CHILD

This other model is based both on studies of effective classroom practice and on years of detailed research on how and in what ways human children learn. Particular notice is taken of how they first learn to speak. Babies and young children have been closely observed in their homes and in their different cultures. Their first utterances, sentences, mutterings, games and reactions have been systematically recorded in texts and contexts. Different conditions for the infant learner have been created and tested.

Through these various studies cognition, that is learning and knowing in human beings, has become recognized as an *active* process closely organized around *affect*. We learn because we are emotional beings, and what we learn and how we learn is closely related to how and what we desire, fear, sense, feel. In his book *Acts of Meaning* Jerome Bruner[4] describes the limitations of a cognitive science that attempted to model the human brain with a computer; only the information-processing activity could be simulated, and even then it was unsatisfactory. Action based on belief, desire and moral commitment could not be modelled or understood. The processing of information is a profoundly different matter to the construction of meaning. When I watch the 2-year-old next door working with his parents in the garden I see and hear him emotionally and intellectually engaged: 'Robbie put stones here... No, no... little stones... these Robbie's stones... put flowers there... Robbie's stones... No, no.' Robbie reacts to everyone who enters the garden. He has worked out an emotional hierarchy for himself and through applying this canonical knowledge (who counts in the hierarchy) he is teaching himself what a garden is. So he is actively engaged in applying concepts, but he is working in relation to other people and his feelings about them. What is fascinating is how he applies *textual* knowledge to the business in hand. 'Mummy say put stones there', he states, before putting the stones somewhere else. Mummy I'm afraid to say does not rate high in his reference system. When she disagrees he becomes furious: 'Daddy say these Robbie's stones.'

In his famous study of children learning language and using language to learn,[5] Gordon Wells pointed to this *active* making of meaning. He also pointed to the centrality of rich and constant home literacy practices in children's achievement in school. Thus, he brought recognition of the activity and emotion of cognition together with textual knowledge as vital in terms of the individual child's intellectual growth. But he showed that this textual behaviour is learned inside a continuous, active construction of meaning.

Another related facet of cognition which also emerges from recent studies is that it is an holistic process, in that specific centres of activity of the human brain are not 'switched on' like light bulbs when we are solving problems, but electrical activity runs through the whole brain. When we read or write, so engaging meaningfully with texts inside a web of social understandings and emotions, we actually employ every bit of our brains.

Many attempts have been made to break down complex cognitive tasks, such as reading, into a series of skills and sub-skills and then reconstruct the task as a descriptive model, one which was then supposed to represent a distinct piece of brain apparatus which could be specifically and separately trained. But, in fact, recent studies have shown that cognitive processes, such as problem-solving and reading, create electrical impulses across the whole brain. The fragmentation involved in setting out a skills-based model of problem-solving to represent reading has become so complex and so variable that no universal agreed structure can be established.

Most importantly for the literacy learner, cognition has also been acknowledged as *enculturated*, that is, all learning and perceiving by an individual is embedded and shaped in a particular and specific culture. Our culturally adapted way of life depends on shared meanings and shared concepts, and on shared modes of discourse for negotiating differences in meaning and interpretation. As Bruner points out, a child 'does not enter the life of his or her group as a private and autistic sport of primary processes, but rather as a participant in a larger public process in which public meanings are negotiated'.[6] Shirley Brice Heath's classic study of different literacy practices in three communities in the USA[7] shows how different children come to language and literacy and also how the multiple ways that texts are presented to them are patterned and deeply enculturated, ways which build particular community understandings and poetics. Literacy is not a neutral technology for children in those different communities any more than it is for different genders, classes or ethnic communities in Britain. Many matters which, traditionally, have been assumed in Britain as universal common sense (the accepted different abilities of women to men, for example), have been shown by cross-cultural research to be merely local habits of mind. Language itself, and particularly literate forms, are deeply enculturated, and so the growing child – active, emotional, fully engaged in learning – is learning, principally through language, what it is to *be* in his or her particular culture and circumstances.

What do we mean by learning how to be? Is this not something which every child learns naturally? To a large extent it is, in that children are natural meaning makers, they are naturally emotional and human. They are aware, too, that they are learning how to perform in a vast variety of differing cultural and social situations. When a 6-year-old I know was asked by her teacher recently what she felt she was learning by playing in the home corner, which was temporarily rigged out as a shop, she answered wisely: 'I am learning *how to be* in a shop.' It seems straightforward, but consciousness formation in a highly literate, industrial society is a contested area, particularly as children grow and change. Access to empowering behaviours, discourses and modes of thought is not, for many children, going to happen naturally; it is intimately bound up with the deliberate educative processes that adults put them through, the texts that they meet, the messages they are given. Consciousness formation is at the root of the arguments and ideologies of official schooling, although the discourse is usually articulated in terms of skills. But skills, as we know, can be learned and unlearned quite easily, depending on the meaning structure and motivation of the learner. If they are oriented to using a knife and fork, to riding a bicycle, to typing, carving, building a brick wall, that is, if they perceive these skills as important and meaningful, then enormous numbers of people will learn them easily and quickly. But *the practices of reading and writing, on the other hand, challenge the ways we want our children to be,* the people we want them to grow into. A model of literacy teaching which openly and explicitly cuts with consciousness formation is perhaps always going to be contested, as it deals in the powers and meanings of texts and messages, not in mechanical exercises. Power and authority in written language is then always open to critical scrutiny.

This more complex model of learning soon challenged the received 'common-sense' view of schooled literacy teaching both from a practical point of view and also from an ideological one. Starting with the practical, it was shown that with speech, even the youngest child learns language in *interaction*, bringing its own will, desires and ideas to an exchange of meanings. For this vital interaction to be optimally educative, the adult speaker has to treat the child's communicative intentions as meaningful and to respond to that meaning. When a toddler says 'Me drink', the best reaction from a language learning point of view is for the adult to respond to the intended meaning: 'Would you like milk or orange juice?', or something similar. Strangely enough, most adults who care for young children do react to meaning naturally, in spite of infelicities of the child's grammar. In this way, through a consistent and collaborative exchange of meanings, the infant child experiments, reorganizes, enriches, practises, improves.

What is important about these early experiences . . . these

interactional episodes provide a framework within which he can discover some of the fundamental principles upon which language in use is based – the reciprocal exchange of signals, the sequential patterning of turns, the assumption of intentionality.[8]

If spoken language, with its complex patterning and variety of registers, is clearly learned in interaction, particularly in collaboration with adult speakers who take time and care to tailor their exchanges to their appreciation of the infant child's growing consciousness, it becomes reasonable to investigate whether or not literacy learning, in spite of the graded exercises handed out to children, is actually most efficiently acquired in a similar way to speech, that is, through *affective and collaborative interaction*. Studies which looked closely at young literacy learners soon pointed out that, even with regard to this highly symbolic code, most if not all children have indeed been interacting with it, actively, for several years before formal schooling. For most pre-school children, stories and poems have already yielded insights into its different patterning and its pleasurable potential, lending a framework of interpretive principles and desires. In addition, environmental print, written language which surrounds our children from birth – road signs, advertisements, lists and messages – has, for nearly all pre-school children, already laid down a cultural and patterned understanding of how writing works in use, before they reach the age of 5.

This knowledge, together with an understanding of how speech is acquired, forms the basis for a more complex view of a young child's emergent literacy. Instead of regarding the child as totally ignorant and in need of instruction, the role of the teacher could change to one of being an assistant and guide in the child's obviously growing mastery of a range of literate forms. Hours spent on wasteful and inappropriate instruction could be used in tailoring literate texts and challenges to each individual child's growing consciousness and desires. Energy previously expended on 'discipline' could be directed to collaborative interaction between the literate adult and the emergent-literate child, sharing and discussing texts and meanings. Texts themselves could thus 'teach' the learner to unlock further ones.[9]

As this different view of the child learner became built into classroom practice, cracking the code of written symbols by young children was found to happen more easily, more naturally, more quickly and more efficiently where a literate adult worked collaboratively with the child learner. In this model, the knowledge and emotion the learner brings to the exchange is respected by both parties. Reading becomes a collaborative event, a sharing of stories and meanings. Writing becomes another shared activity, a grasping for and appreciation of literate expression. Children learn to put down their own thoughts in writing as drafts and then, through sharing them with the teacher and with each other, to edit and improve their work and ideas. They learn to study and consider different forms of literature and use its genres for their own purposes. In this well-tried model literacy is thus learned through affective experimentation, where symbolic skills are developed in the effort of making meaning. In homes and classrooms where this model is in place, children continuously build on what they know through allowable, pleasurable, imaginative and various experimentation. They make mistakes, create nonsense, discuss their writings, revise, elaborate, discard, edit and rewrite in an atmosphere of imaginative and appreciative encouragement. The obvious effectiveness of this approach, in terms of the learning and literate empowerment of the individual child, was demonstrated and celebrated in Britain during the years of the National Writing Project, from 1985 to 1989, when children's writing began to make a dramatic impact on educational thought in terms of its quality and quantity. Since then, however, this model of teaching literacy has been under almost continuous attack from outside schools, principally from a Conservative government, presumably with the intention of restoring authority through and in language and literature teaching over a potentially iconoclastic and effectively outspoken young population.

NEW LITERACIES, NEW LEARNING: PROBLEMS AND POSSIBILITIES

Because of a commitment to this more developed and effective model of teaching and learning, teachers soon felt embattled in relation to some of the more myopic and authoritarian demands of the National Curriculum in English imposed on them from 'above'. Written standard English, the epitome of the schooled model of literacy, has been put in place above the spoken dialectal forms of English many child learners bring to the classroom. Mastery of this form of English is 'assessed' very early in the child's school life, thus yielding an enormous advantage to middle-class children who speak this form of English at home, and thereby 'naturalizing' its class basis and marginalizing the richness of expression of working-class and ethnic dialectal forms. Literacy learning in the early years has begun to come under pressure to return to the old instructional model, with secretarial features of writing (full stops and capital letters by the age of 6) given enormous and futile prominence in new assessment procedures. All this has been put in place in the teeth of the cultural fact that imaginative writing for television and film, where a variety of vernacular and dialectal forms of English is increasingly valued, is one of the most important forms in maintaining and reflecting the wide variations and subtle nuances of British cultural life. And also in spite of the knowledge that confidence and mastery of any new form of self-expression, from standard English to Shakespearean drama, starts with inner self-esteem, intimately bound up with a confidence in one's own dialectal mother tongue and its development within a community of speakers.

However, despite the burden of these ideological and administrative pressures, some of the recent problems that teachers face with encouraging active learning in language and literacy are often to do with the effects and interests of the children's cultural world 'outside'. Building collaboratively and effectively on each child's growing grasp of literate behaviour means admitting the child's voice and thoughts into the classroom as a legitimate and respected part of growing consciousness and it becoming the central cultural material with which to work. This can lead sometimes to dramatic and, what teachers perceive as, crudely unpleasant and even depraved texts and messages being admitted to the heart of the curriculum. It can open up areas of children's cultural lives which are alarmingly unchildish and apparently morally unsuitable: sexual, adult, racial and violent. More frequently, however, there is a large emotional and imaginative investment made by children in narratives and cultural material invented for them by an industry which has lately successfully targeted child consumers outside school. Linking new forms of communication technology, such as videos and computer games, to exciting and satisfying stories has created a huge cultural challenge to the book culture of the school English curriculum. There can be no question as to the highly developed visual literacy, the ability to 'read' the narratives of film and the iconography of comics, advertisement and cartoons that children bring with them into school. But what they read, and how they read, in a new era of video, comic book and computer game availability now presents new and exciting challenges on a vast scale to the teacher who believes that texts, rather than mechanical skills, are central to learning.

So a model of the learner which incorporates developed abilities and seeks to develop consciousness through building collaboratively on his or her prior knowledge can lead to a problematic teaching role. Moral issues, kept tidily, if ultimately dangerously, under the carpet by the application of an authoritarian model of schooled literacy, spring into almost unmanageable prominence with a collaborative approach. The myth of literacy as a neutral technology becomes exposed, as issues of gender are now seen as deeply embedded in differing literate practices. My two most prolific 7-year-old story writers were Karen and Mark. Karen wrote continually about 'Princess Sarah', who was not only beautiful in an obvious Barbie doll image (tall, fair and with an elaborate series of outfits) but this heroine always 'made friends' with everyone, inviting them into her castle for cups of tea. Mark's heroes, meanwhile, were continually fighting, scarcely a breath between kneeing, punching, flattening, 'slicing their eyeballs' and 'smashing their guts'. I could not move either of them from these highly gendered positions as writers and, like many teachers, I was unsure whether I should attempt to do so because their narratives were clearly 'borrowed' from cultural sources outside school and writing them clearly gave both children considerable pleasure. Karen appeared to embrace without question what, to me, appeared the saccharine inanities of her favourite comics for girls – *Twinkle* and *My Little Pony* – whilst Mark reproduced some of the, to me, unpleasant and mindless violence from his brother's computer games.

If issues of gender become open to scrutiny through encouraging children to write in their own voices, then issues of class and ethnicity soon emerge which completely overturn any residual idea that literacy is a neutral technology which can somehow be impartially distributed through instruction. Ethnographic studies of what literacy is and how it is integrated with social practices, particularly child-rearing and community moralities, have pointed to its vastly varying potentialities. Access to cultural goods in our society is not equally distributed, and the social practices of different classes, communities and families, of which literate practices are one facet, quickly point up where the child stands in relation to power, particularly power in language. This social positioning in relation to power is reflected in the children's choices of texts, the ways they approach writing and knowledge, the views they have of their own abilities and futures. Here again the sensitive teacher becomes crucial in helping each child to unlock further texts and improve his or her power over the written word and through it to achieve a wider intellectual grasp and sense of diversity. Working with consciousness can make vital differences both to cultural practices and the empowering of young learners by *meaningful* introduction of particular and relevant new texts and ways of thinking. To introduce texts which are salient for the learner, which challenge his or her subjectivity and which build on pleasure, is to engage the pupil in deep thinking. To do this, each teacher has to understand and appreciate the activity, the emotion and the enculturation of cognition in individual children. In addition, it is necessary to consider the ways in which all texts, from videos, books and comics are constructed, to study the particular ways each text and genre yields pleasure, and to work towards a deeper understanding of the active manner in which they are read. It must be acknowledged that the popular culture industry for children is various and often clumsy, but it works hard to understand the grain of desire and consequently many of its texts and messages yield considerable delight. If we wish to unlock further texts for children we must get inside the ways they are already making meaning and getting pleasure from the products of an industry which is ultimately aimed, not to enlarge consciousness, but to make profits for its shareholders.

It must also be acknowledged that most children are not only sophisticated readers in a technical sense of the popular culture narratives aimed at children, that is, they appear to be able to understand form, story, nuance, detail, intention with pictures and animated film, with image and live-action, but they can use these narratives and replay them to give themselves satisfaction. Going further than this, they desire the toys and artefacts that the culture industry also provides and thus they create considerable demands as consumers. Narrative desire, which works directly on the imagination, can be a powerful force in their cultural lives. Mothers have told me how they have been desperately nagged, sometimes going without an important item for themselves like a winter coat so they can afford to buy their desirous child the latest toy figure. With the toy the child becomes an agent and author of his or her own desires, playing out pleasurable narratives again and again. This kind of activity, the watching of narratives and the imaginative playing to extend their pleasure is, this book argues, connected intimately with the educative pleasure of reading literature – both are presenting the child with texts which affect consciousness and both are therefore the vital cultural material that the literacy teacher deals in. If we develop a critical vocabulary and an appreciation of the multi-levelled complexity of this activity, if we can bring ourselves to better understand this play, we can use its richness and potential to make exciting bridges to lead children to written texts.

So this book attempts to look at many of these considerable forces at work in children's cultural lives and to consider the role of the teacher and of literature in relation to them. It examines these new phenomena in detail and offers some ways of thinking, some theoretical tools that could be useful. It places a high value on the work teachers already do with children, describes the sympathy and imagination they expend, and shows how vital their hard work is. It opens with two chapters which discuss the current situation and which offer a variety of theoretical approaches to help grasp its complexity and possibilities. The following two chapters focus on empirical work with children in primary schools, from the early years to the middle years. These chapters examine in detail some of the cultural and social processes that children are engaged in and demonstrate some of the exciting links teachers can make using the narratives of popular culture as a shared context for developing work with other texts in the classroom. The final two chapters trace different paths of boys and girls as they enter adolescence, young teenagers who are seeking ways of integrating the pleasures and fantasies of the popular into their growing adult subjectivities alongside the strongly developed cultures of home and school. Although the book presents features of a developmental narrative with regard to age and attitude, the point is really to emphasize not one 'story' of growth and change, but rather to suggest that many of the same processes are at work across the ages of official childhood.

So a central theme emerges in the book which beckons to a deeper respect for the narrative desires of children and a greater appreciation of their sophisticated activity when engaged with the products of the culture industry. These young active meaning makers do need the help of their teachers to further their knowledge and delight in texts and to offer them guidance towards the deep pleasures of engagement with literature. Understanding what gives them pleasure, developing a critical vocabulary which embraces the constructedness of media texts, watching them use fantasy to construct their own complicated and multifaceted, yet integrated adult subjectivities, sympathizing with the efforts they have to make to blossom into a rich and empowering literacy and helping them understand the powerful pleasures that can be enjoyed through books as well as visual narratives, each literacy providing potent possibilities and engaging with desire, is, this book argues, the role of the teacher for this new wise generation.

NOTES

1 David Vincent, *Literacy and Popular Culture: England 1750–1914*, Cambridge: Cambridge University Press, 1989, p. 91 (my italics).
2 Vincent, op. cit., p. 273.
3 Scarcely a week has passed over the last ten years without an article suggesting that children are not being taught to read properly in the *Sunday Times, Daily Mail*, etc.
4 Jerome Bruner, *Acts of Meaning*, Cambridge Mass.: Harvard University Press, 1990.
5 Gordon Wells, *The Meaning Makers: Children Learning Language and Using Language to Learn*, London: Hodder & Stoughton, 1986.
6 Bruner, op. cit., p. 13.
7 Shirley Brice Heath, *Ways With Words: Language, Life and Work in Communities and Classrooms*, Cambridge: Cambridge University Press, 1983.
8 Gordon Wells and John Nicholls (eds), *Language and Learning: An Interactional Perspective*, Lewes: The Falmer Press, 1985, p. 24.
9 Margaret Meek, *How Texts Teach what Readers Learn*, London: Thimble Press, 1990.

FURTHER READING

In addition to the books cited, here are some further books on the nature of literacy in society.

Graff, Harvey J., *The Labyrinths of Literacy*, Lewes: The Falmer Press, 1987.

Lankshear, Colin with Lawler, Moira, *Literacy, Schooling and Revolution*, Lewes: The Falmer Press, 1987.

Maybin, Janet (ed.), *Language and Literacy in Social Practice: A Reader*, Avon: Multilingual Matters, 1994.

Meek, Margaret, *On Being Literate*, London: The Bodley Head, 1991.

Street, Brian, *Literacy in Theory and Practice*, Cambridge: Cambridge University Press, 1984.

Wells, Gordon and Nicholls, John (eds), *Language and Learning: An Interactional Perspective*, Lewes: The Falmer Press, 1985.

There are several good books on the ideology of language and gender. Two interesting ones are:

Steedman, Carolyn, *The Tidy House*, London: Virago, 1983.

Steedman, Carolyn, Urwin, Cathy and Walkerdine, Valerie (eds), *Language, Gender and Childhood*, London: Routledge & Kegan Paul, 1985.

Part I

Ways of looking

In the first two chapters we consider in detail the ways the popular culture industry works to interest children and consider the many various ways children derive pleasure from its products and stories. In Chapter 1 I look at the history of the steadily growing pervasiveness and profits of the toy and media industry over this century. I describe how new communication technologies such as comic books, animation, television and now video began to reach directly the imaginations of children without the mediation of taught literacy, without them having to read and write in traditional ways. Because children wish to play as agents and authors of their own narrative pleasures, this has led to vast profits being generated from lucrative product licensing by companies such as the Disney Corporation and Warner Brothers with toys and games based on their video narratives. I explore some of the educational implications of this cultural phenomenon, bringing to them two different but linked interpretations, first, a 'cultural feminist' interpretation of the inherent sexism in the popular culture industry and, second, a psychodynamic interpretation which looks at why children appear to desire and accept these highly gendered forms of the narratives and products. I use this latter theoretical account to suggest how teachers may confidently work with narrative desire, understanding how the plots of stories often address deep gender and cultural anxieties and therefore yield considerable pleasure, but that narrative desire is also invested in other forms and often resides strongly in the rich details of context in which many stories are embedded. It is here, in understanding gendered narratives, seeing where they connect with literature, and in enriching the contextual landscape through imaginative topic work that, I argue, the possibilities for change and the eventual empowerment of the children's own stories lie.

In Chapter 2 David Whitley looks in depth at the ways children read and get pleasure from media narratives. Because, as he argues, children's experience is now embedded in a wealth of these narratives, this can pose a potential obstacle for many teachers, as often children's writing may seem to be dominated by wholesale borrowings of media themes, plots and scenarios if these are admitted in a positive way. If, on the other hand, media experience is excluded as low-grade or irrelevant, many children find difficulty in engaging with a syllabus which fails to address what is important to them. Is this, he asks, a necessary dichotomy. Taking as his starting point a conceptual framework derived from media studies, he explores different ways of thinking about children's experience of media narratives which could enable these to be incorporated in more positive forms in the classroom. In particular, he argues that the degree to which children regard events within media narratives as 'real' – which is related to what media theorists define as the modality of particular sequences – is of critical importance in determining attitude and response. Through examining these processes of perception we may also be able to develop a richer critical vocabulary to share with children when discussing media narratives, leading to more productive engagement with these potent fictions in the classroom.

Chapter 1

Manufacturing make-believe
Notes on the toy and media industry for children

Mary Hilton

Right from the moment of birth the popular culture industry appears to place different narratives around the male and female body; from the cards welcoming the new baby in pink for girls and blue for boys, to the first little dolls that speak of motherhood and beauty for girls, and little toolkits and toy cars which speak of action and technology for boys. Soon, through videos and comics, through different clothing and artefacts, eventually to pulp fiction and teen magazines, the industry produces a highly gendered range of stories and images that point to different roles, different concerns, different areas of adult competence for the growing boy and girl. To what extent are these gendered narratives and artefacts coercive or salient? In what ways have the old ways of reading been transformed and new ways been introduced to help make enormous profits for an industry that now targets children as consumers from the first growth of consciousness, from the first moments of considering who they are? Most importantly, why do children appear to *desire* both the stories and the toys? In opening this book on the nature and challenge of popular culture for children, these are the questions this chapter addresses.

PRIMARY PROCESSES – THE TOY AND THE STORY

As far back in history as we can survey, children have played with toys. In Western culture the rattle, said to be invented by Archytas, was the first toy of the ancient Greek child, then painted clay puppets representing human beings or animals, houses or ships made of leather and other toys made by the children themselves were commonly enjoyed.[1] Then, as now, through play with toys, children rehearsed and reassembled the important narratives of their culture, taking different roles, creating different possibilities. Now, as then, small figures, whether they are dolls, soldiers, ponies, warriors, animals from the Ark or a zoo, are manipulated by small hands and set in different postures; they are put to bed, thrown huge distances, tucked into pockets and bags; in time-worn ways they are loved, drowned, beheaded, cuddled, smacked, forgotten, rescued. And through these active and dramatic processes a private fictional world is created, sustained and explored. Teachers of young children respect and have helped to enrich these private worlds by filling their classrooms with books and stories. Writers for children have engaged in this deep play of imagination and desire with tempting and complex narratives, extending the child's range of fictional possibilities, roles and reactions. Many adults consider that story and play, although often private and primitive in childhood, are rooted in the same instincts, spring from the same creative sources and exhibit the same constructions which are articulated and embellished as literature and theatre in the adult and public domain.

To many teachers and educators children's early imaginative play is, then, considered of immense importance. Long before 'play therapists' began to point to its therapeutic properties for disturbed or anxious children, the great educational theorists of the early nineteenth century, Pestalozzi and Froebel, believed that children learned through play, particularly free imaginative play. The distinguished educationalist of our own time, Jerome Bruner, pointed to two forms of thought: the *paradigmatic* and the *narrative*. The first is the ability to think in orderly logical sequences; the second the ability to mirror events, to form them into stories and to create possible worlds as the bases for action.[2] Many educators believe that the early make-believe play of children is the beginning of the development of this narrative thought.[3]

Throughout the nineteenth century children's books were often sold with a toy as an imaginative package for the child. The idea was presumably current then that a small figure to play with allowed the child creatively to extend the possibilities of the written story. Today, still, a manufactured toy figure sold with a narrative is an invitation to play, but one which, as we know, often is scarcely needed, as children play anyway, usually becoming themselves the protagonists of the story. And with young children the imaginative schema in play is wrapped so powerfully with fantasy that the material 'look' or even 'feel' of a play object can sometimes seem extraordinarily inappropriate to an adult eye. If a little girl or boy wishes to mother and nothing else is available, they will mother even a stick or a plastic skittle; if they wish to stage a fight they will set a pencil against a teapot. When a narrative fantasy of gripping intensity is running through the child's head, the material configuration is apparently of minor importance:

> Magic weaves in and out of everything the children say and do. The boundaries between what the child thinks and what the adult sees are never clear to the adult, but the child does not expect compatibility. The child himself is the ultimate magician.[4]

But what cunning toymakers have realized for over a century is that the imaginative tide can run the other way too, from the material to the fantastic.

With the advent of a huge range of toys and artefacts for children and huge profits to be made, many controversies now centre around this basic consensus which puts the narrative play of children at the centre of educative processes. The main one concerns itself with the nature of the play environment, particularly *which* toys we give our children to play with. Many toys appear to represent cultural narratives which are often highly, not to say oppressively, gendered. For example, the vast toy retail exhibition held every year in Olympia, London shows a breathtaking division in views of the young female and young male body and associated play activities, materializing the particular cultural apparatus of a highly gendered world for the appreciation and desire of very young children. A world where pink, plastic, soft, static, 'caring' toys for girls are in sharp contrast to the vast range of aggressive, militarist, technical and moving toys for boys. Soft pink plastic flesh, long, blonde artificial hair, lacy pink and pastel clothing, jewellery, hairdressing equipment, cosmetics and miniature household equipment, toy dream homes, all seem to pin girls into a static consumerist fantasy which openly declares that the Western female body is an object of sexual and sensual gratification, ready to be stroked and adorned within an enhancing milieu of soft yet sparkling material fabrics. The male body and its associated play activities are, by contrast, active and destructive. The boys' toys speak of endless physical attack on the body: bombing, punching, flattening, kicking, together with a phantasmagorical array of monstrous bodily hideosity in the grotesque 'enemy' figures of aliens and mutants. The bodies of the heroes are also stereotyped: hard and lean, with plastic articulations which form aggressive postures. Masculinity is here being constructed out of a constant story of bodily and technological conflict.

Where have these stereotyped plastic figures come from and how have the stories on which they are based reached the imaginations of so many children, providing for their manufacturers such a vast and lucrative industry?

IDEALIZED CHILDHOOD IN VICTORIAN BRITAIN

For over a hundred years toy manufacturers have shaped their small figures according to the popular social narratives of the day. Traditionally, in early nineteenth-century Britain little girls were given dolls as part of a narrative linking femininity and motherhood, and little boys were given toy soldiers as a constitutive part of the powerful story of the militarist might of the imperial nation. By the mid-nineteenth century, a Romantic ideology of childhood, linking children with nature and creating a fictional pastoral space in which children were ideally free to roam and grow, had entered and become widespread in middleclass cultural life. This was reflected in a generic shift in stories for young children, where animals became intertwined in domestic and kindly narratives of contained liberality. These were in stark contrast to the retributive and moralistic evangelical stories for children of an earlier generation. Lewis Carroll's *Alice in Wonderland*, published in 1865, introduced a series of beautifully delineated friendly character animals that helped and hindered the young heroine. Later again, in the early twentieth century, such children's classics as Kenneth Grahame's *The Wind in the Willows*, and Beatrix Potter's *Peter Rabbit* created gentle narratives from a middle-class and conservative perspective in a somewhat paradoxical[5] but convincing animality. By using the small native animals of the countryside – the rabbit, toad, mouse, mole and badger – as protagonists, the delights of comfortable domesticity could be developed within a nostalgic, pastoral existence, smoothing away problematic issues of class and inequality in the growing urban world and, at the same time, regulating and transforming the savage mindlessness of the natural world. Out of this combination of the upper-middle-class nursery and idealized animality came the classic humanoid of English childhood – the teddy bear – male, tubby, naive, lovable. He was to be immortalized in literature for children by A. A. Milne in *Winnie the Pooh*. In Britain the teddy bear has been a best-selling plush toy for over half a century.

Marina Warner, in her Reith lectures in 1994, pointed to the dangers of the mythology of childish innocence which grew up in Britain in the late nineteenth century. To her, as well as to Kimberly Reynolds[6] and Carolyn Steedman[7] the idealized and sexless child came to represent the adult's own interiority, our own lost innocence, helping us shed our cynicism and resistance to the knowledge of the selves and the society we have made: 'The nagging, yearning desire to work back to a pristine state of goodness, an Eden of lost innocence, has focussed on children.'[8] In reality, during this period up to the First World War childhood for most children was poverty-bound and short. It was the growing bourgeoisie that laid down, through their 'classics', through their stories and images, a picture of an idealized child which was innocent, tender, dreamy and gentle. This idealized vision was widely to affect social attitudes to children and childhood after the First World War. It was continuously to challenge the texts presented to children. It underlay the times of moral panic and, according to Warner, created the dangerous myth that children are somehow 'different', not only beautiful but *potentially evil*. She believes there still lives in society a helpless suspicion that children may look like angels but be devils underneath. Our culture still 'plays' with this myth of idealized and innocent childhood in which it has embedded and invested both desire – for our own lost tender innocence – and fear – that the pristine goodness for which we yearn might never have existed in the first place.

As a result, children's growing sexuality had been consistently ignored in classic literature for children, although I believe it has lain masked but active in many popular texts to which they have often seemed 'unhealthily' attracted. As new forms of iconographic texts were developed after the First World War, comics and films for children, to which the growing and consuming child had direct access, so too did ideas of 'childhood' become increasingly contested both in Britain and in America. Many of the areas of contest seemed again to threaten the pervasive image of idealized and innocent childhood and how it should be shaped and set apart from adulthood.

CINEMA AND COMIC BOOK – NEW LITERACIES, NEW GENRES

In the 1930s in America two new narrative mediums for children were invented and propagated: the animated film and the comic book, linking new pictorial literacies through new forms of mass-production directly to the child consumer. By this I mean that the story was no longer written and read using the traditional literacy practices of writing and reading words, and therefore young 'pre-literate' children could be brought within consumer culture, catered for and directly considered as subjects with particular and identifiable tastes and desires. And soon within these new pictorial media for children there opened up two new images of immense popularity, the animated animal and the male superhero, materialized and epitomized in what were to become national icons: Mickey Mouse and Superman.

Walt Disney's Mickey Mouse films intensified a complex set of debates about the role of cinema in children's lives. According to Richard deCordova in a recent book about the Disney Corporation:

> During the late 1920's and early 1930's the cinema's address to children was contested ground and a matter of frenzied concern. Reformers denounced the movies' influence on children and mounted well organized efforts across the country to regulate and control this aspect of children's leisure. One particular important aspect of these efforts was the creation and supervision of a canon of films for children ... Disney's films entered and achieved a privileged position in this canon ... In Mickey Mouse, the cultural interests of children, the interests of the film industry, and the political interests of reformers seemed merged. And today, something

like a sacred connection exists in Mickey Mouse and idealized childhood.[9]

In his fascinating analysis of early child consumer culture in America deCordova shows that during the early decades of this century, as today, there was an enormous cultural investment in association of childhood with animality. The new emphasis on play closely linked the toy and film industry, and Disney's animated animals served to consolidate the idea of an innocent and educative play fiction for children.

In addition to Mickey Mouse's debut, which linked animation animality and childhood in American culture, establishing over-night a fortune for his creator, deCordova points out that from the late 1920s there was an intensification and rationalization of the industrial and marketing processes whereby films were linked to consumer goods:

> Such organizations as Hollywood Fashion Associates and the Modern Merchandising Bureau emerged to co-ordinate the display of fashions in Hollywood films and fan magazines with the subsequent production and marketing of those fashions. And the studio departments systematically began to conceive of story ideas and scripts as opportunities for a wider range of lucrative product tie-ins ... These develop-ments consolidated the cinema's role as a force in the rise of American consumerism ... The Disney Company was at the forefront of these innovations in the early 1930s ... a vast array of Mickey Mouse dolls, toys and novelty items pro-duced from 1930 on sold ... to an appreciative and generally young public.[10]

Also in the 1930s in America another technological break-through had been achieved, creating a new medium to reach the narrative imagination of the 'non-literate' child. Comic books began as reprints of comic strips from newspapers and the medium quickly became children's fare. It utilized a cheap format so it could be printed regularly in a magazine rack for distributions. The first comic book series really to succeed was *Action Comics*, with Superman appearing in its first issue in 1938. The superhero rage in America was thus started by a man who wore his underpants outside his tights but, apart from this unusual quirk, no aspect of his character was completely new;

it was their combination in one complete imaginary being that was without precedent.

Schuster's first rendering of the character included the description: 'A genius in intellect. A Hercules in strength. A Nemesis for wrongdoers.'

As sales went up producers tailored their products to what sold and who bought – Superheroes sold and children bought ... As it expanded, the medium picked up another characteristic that distinguished it. Companies began to establish unified and recognizable universes throughout their products, providing their readers with clearly identifiable, coherent fictional worlds which were also a company's 'brand' identities. Company identity was tied to the type of adventure that was sold.[11]

Superman's natural arena for his particular intellect and strength was the growing crime in the American city. Any interesting weakness in the character or demeanour of the historical and legendary hero was expunged, leaving a fictional character that could simply overcome, immediately, by the process of brute force, any evil-doer or participant in inner city crime. This somewhat two-dimensional notion of the American child's superhero still seems to work successfully with the fantasy desires of the young male child, obliterating complications of personality and individuality. As Vivian Gussin Paley observed with her 5-year-olds:

Superhero drama is dynamic and satisfying, but ... the only change came about through bringing in a new superhero or killing more bad guys. The stories [of the boys] do not reflect the qualities of a particular child or encourage variations ... Such stories are used to mask, not reveal, individuality.[12]

Only one other superhero was to rival Superman in importance: Batman. And when, in the 1950s, the American public turned on the superheroes and debarred them for children it was Batman's more complex and psychologically interesting persona which gave greatest concern:

Batman as a feature, was infinitely better plotted, better villained, better looking than Superman. Batman inhabited a world where no-one, whatever the time of day, cast any thing but long shadows – seen from weird perspectives. Batman's world was scarey, Superman's never.[13]

So Batman's enormous strength was not like Superman's – a straightforward device for bringing the child into the drama – it was rather his psychological plausibility which permeated the character in his world which attempted to draw in the child reader. Here, the innocence of childhood was more dramatically put to the test. There is something sophisticated, almost sinister, in his life of vengeance and the shadowy way it is constructed.

Superman and other superheroes did not have a straight-forward success-story history within American culture, however. Although during the Second World War the sky thickened with superheroes and their villainous 'ratzi' enemies, as the comic book industry continued to grow after the war it was attacked by psychologists, parents and senate committees. They were all shocked by the apparently 'adult' themes appearing in a medium they perceived as exclusively for children. During the early 1950s and the McCarthyite era the superheroes and the comic books were under perpetual attack. PTAs, community watchdog groups and the media joined this chorus. Juvenile crime was linked to comic books and the superheroes. Dr Frederic Wertham, influential senior psychiatrist from the New York Department of Hospitals, charged that comic books undermined morals, glorified violence and were sexually aggressive in an abnormal way. His most damaging assertion was that reading comic books was a distinct influencing factor in every single delinquent or disturbed child he had studied. Wertham connected comic books with every kind of social and moral perversion, including sadism, theft, murder and rape. Wertham had a special distaste for superheroes who, he claimed, undermined respect for the law in decent citizens.[14] Here again, the innocence of children seemed at risk but with a new aspect to the difficulties, not just the child as a commodity, but the child as a consumer. Childhood sexuality, it seemed, would have to be contained by censorship, if the category of 'not adult' was to retain any power to contain the continuing emotional and financial investment by the adult world.

PLASTIC, TELEVISION AND VIDEO – WORLDS OF FANTASY AND PROFIT

In spite of this moral pressure on the nature of superheroes and their temporary withdrawal from the market-place, the vast industrial and organizational commercial groundwork which linked toy products with imaginary characters from the pens of illustrators and animators, directly reaching the imaginations of children without the traditional mediation of schooled literacy, was laid before the Second World War. After the War, by the 1950s, two important technological innovations, widely changing both the imaginative and material circumstances of Western domestic and cultural living, enhanced and embellished the growing toy and media industry beyond the wildest expectations. These innovations were television and plastic.

As home television quickly became widespread in Britain in the mid- and late 1950s, the toy industry began to invest in advertising, showing a range of traditional toys for boys, such as train sets and toolkits and less frequently doll and play outfits for girls. Soon it was realized that this medium could be used, not simply to display products but to set up developed narrative ideas in children's minds. Chad Valley made the first television advertisements for toys in the mid-1950s, and now, as then, television adverts still play a crucial role in most toy marketing successes.[15] In addition, plastic – cheap, durable, safer and highly coloured – could replace the dolls that had hitherto been made of celluloid and porcelain. Celluloid was highly combustible and porcelain breakable. Plastic also replaced tin plate as the material most used for general toys such as model vehicles and spinning tops. Its use enabled the British toy industry in 1961 to produce a set of toy safety standards to overcome the previous problems of lead poisoning, burning and choking hazards which had been perpetual problems in the industry. Many toys produced before plastic use became widespread would fail today's safety tests.

By the early 1960s the superheroes had quietly returned, but their arena of recognizable moral and physical superiority had been transformed from the global and urban to the stellar and mythical. Structures of the violent crime story had been removed from their worryingly 'adult' connotations of sexual and realistic inner city detail and had been developed to colonize a new mythical universe of outer space. The imperialist vision inherent in the adventure story, combined with the staggering financial and emotional national investment in American space technology, helped to initiate a new and exciting fictional genre. The hard lean bodies of 'democratic' American conquerors now kept order and instilled civilization in a fantasy universe, full of demons, corrupt regimes, aliens and mutant warriors. New plastic toys could replicate the extraordinary animated figures in previously unbelievable three-dimensional form. Plastic could be moulded, coloured and shaped to model the new rash of space ships, artillery and space stations, keeping a male ideology of techno-muscularity alive and developing amongst small boys as it was amongst men. Later, in the 1980s, Superman and Batman were to stage a comeback, but by then subtly changed, full of ironies and sophisticated play within the genre.

By the 1990s stories of space-age teams of superheroes were still the most popular male narratives for the toy industry. Bandai, which is a partly Japanese company, stitched together some clips and ideas from a Japanese television narrative and invented a group of American superheroes, the *Power Rangers* to combat endlessly a feminine witch, Rita Repulsa, and her evil space aliens. Interestingly, a new Japanese aesthetic of the warrior body, a series of martial arts' and karate postures are built in to the stories and the crafted articulations of the plastic bodies. In addition, there are an increasingly number of female figures within this genre, but these still have to conform to a hard, lean, athletic muscularity in order to cross gender boundaries into superheroship. With the crafted Zords, the warrior body is extended by magic into the realm of technological superiority; the fusion of the images of the body into vast fighting machines is completed with breathtaking wizardry.

From the 1930s Disney had continued to market Mickey and Minnie Mouse, Donald Duck and a host of recognizable Disney animal characters, sticking closely to the original formula of stylized and domesticated animality. By 1940 the cartoons, the principal Disney product, together with a vast range of toys and other childish accoutrements, such as wristwatches, mugs, lamps, etc., reached an increasingly international audience. All the same, in 1948 and 1949 the Disney Company teetered on the brink of insolvency. Live action feature films could not save the company. By the 1960s the Disney Company had shifted its major investment from film making to being a mass culture maker of theme parks and television shows. In this way it regained its old position as a core business in American popular culture. When Walt Disney died in 1966 and his brother Roy 5 years later, the company was to coast along on its established products for two decades. By the 1980s the company had the film unit again adding to corporate profits and had opened two further theme parks, one in California and one in Japan. Euro Disney was planned to open in 1992. By 1990 the pay-TV Disney Channel, through a complicated set of cross-promotions, had 5 million subscribers and began to make money.[16]

However, in the 1990s it was the undreamed of popularity of a new cultural technology that again strengthened the vast Disney profits and tightened its central grip on the popular culture industry for children throughout the Western world – the home video.

By packaging and proffering the classics of Disney animation in the home video market the company added more than $100 million dollars to its pure profit in 1986 alone. *The Lady and the Tramp, Bambi* and *Cinderella* became all-time best sellers on video. Lucrative product licensing, with tough deals made with a whole range of toys and child products again poured money into the Disney coffers, allowing them to write off the losses of Euro Disney and to set themselves the task of creating yet more animated films aimed at children, again with extremely profitable licensing arrangements with toy and artefact manufacturers for a dazzling array of toy figures. Mattel, the toy company that holds the main Disney licence has seen profits soar in the 1990s, with a new release of an animated video providing a narrative context for their new plastic toy figures each year, from *Aladdin* to *The Lion King* and *Pocahontas*.

Mattel, however, already held a lucrative figure in the toy industry; a figure which, in the 1960s was placed to reflect a new post-war image of femininity. For the baby-boomer generation growing up in the 1960s motherhood could be set aside – to demonstrate this, a new figure appeared as an icon of femininity embedded in a powerful modern narrative of consumption. She was going to have an immense array of feminine clothes, bright pink flesh, an adult body and the long blonde-white hair of the all-American girl, complete with boyfriend, tiara and later make-up and hairdressing equipment. She was to represent the shift in an ideology of female motherhood to an ideology of feminine consumer conquest. In 1961 Barbie appeared. According to Bob Dixon in *Playing Them False: A Study of Children's Toys, Games and Puzzles*, fashion dolls, often richly dressed, go back at least to the mid-eighteenth century and were contemporaneous with the first books and board games which were meant specifically for children. But the current pink articulated female figures, aimed specifically at girls between the ages of 6 and 12 – Barbie from Mattel and Sindy from Pedigree (later Hasbro), together make up over 90 per cent of the fashion doll market – are blatant articulations of a feminine consumerist fantasy. Both of them have an existence in fiction: from early 1966 there have been a series of comics and annuals featuring 'stories' about each heroine which are really long series of advertisements. The comic strip, *Sindy's Disaster Day*, for example, has a farcical story but we do see Sindy in seven of her outfits.[17]

Interestingly, Mattel has recently brought the most controversial toy on to the American market. As the baby-boomer generation has moved into grandparenthood Mattel has produced a doll for 3- to 7-year-olds called *My Bundle Baby*. It is a typically spongy, soft doll, 11 inches tall and comes enclosed in a soft carrying bag, like the ones real babies are carried in. When the child first opens the pack they find whether the stork (of which there is a picture) has brought them a boy (dressed in blue) or a girl (in pink). In America there has been widespread condemnation of such a pregnancy plaything.[18] The doll has been considered an invasion of parental rights, a source of dangerous misinformation to the young about pregnancy and likely to create even more unwanted pregnancies in the young teenage sector, already an area of national concern. Again, the boundaries of childhood innocence have been challenged in new and worrying ways.

CONSTRUCTING CHRISTMAS

As an idealized time of childhood emerged during the nineteenth century, in Britain a whole domestic ideology grew up that had its economic foundations in the withdrawal of middle-class women from paid labour. Woman's highest destiny was to be 'the angel in the house', committed to motherhood and the care and moral training of her young children. The retributive wrathful God of the Old Testament, much referred to by the widespread evangelical movement in the early part of the century, became softened and forgiving and there was a new emphasis on the life of Christ in the New Testament around the middle of the century. Likewise, the festival of the celebration of His birth gradually replaced in national activity and importance the theologically more important festival of His death and resurrection. By the mid-Victorian period, Christmas, overlaying the ancient winter solstice, became a time of intense consumer and sentimental focus on the family. From mid-century onwards images of English Christmas, from yule logs, Christmas trees, carol singing, Scrooge, Mr Pickwick, etc. all served to enhance a picture of a time of peace, of a flux of goodwill, a season to focus on the family and particularly on children.

From that time the toy industry accepted and endorsed a strong seasonality in its business. Nearly 70 per cent of all toys are bought in the last quarter of the year, which means however that they must be conceived and made much earlier.[19] Indeed, given the fickleness of childish taste and the relatively high cost of plastic tooling, the toy companies have to set out their goods for retail inspection and purchase in the preceding January. In addition to the risks associated in investment in consumer goods which might not have achieved sufficient popularity in 11 months' time, the toy companies have to work hard at conceiving narratives and concepts often expensively licensed from media companies such as Disney that, released to children over the year, will set certain desires in motion.

There is a timing and a construction about the whole toy business which soon eradicates any notion of a spontaneous and romantic flux in consumer purchasing for children at Christmas. The large toy companies have it all carefully worked out over a year before. First, a narrative video is released in the cinema and then onto the home video market in March, which introduces the new characters powerfully embedded in a story. From May onwards these characters are then released into a television mini-series which brings them regularly before the children. Often a second 'follow-up' video is released onto the home video market, with further adventures. By October the plastic figures are completed and sent to the pre-booked retailers. By November television advertising slots are taken with increasing frequency, adverts which 'remind' the children of the narrative play potential in the particular figures. Many things can, however, go wrong. The media narratives can simply fail to grab the children's interest or imagination. Sometimes the products are too desirable and the retailers have simply not stocked enough. Conversely, last year's narratives can quickly stale, leaving whole runs of figures unsold.

THE CHILD CONSUMER OF STORIES AND TOYS

Many of the features of the toy and media industry, with their close concentration of interests, and their sophisticated knowledge of the child consumer, raise important issues for parents and educators. Until the home video became a universal reality, easily operable by the pre-school child, adult supervision, indeed literate and discursive mediation of the powerful narratives of childhood, could be achieved. Stories had to be written, chosen and purchased in book form and then read aloud to young children. Comics and picture books could be carefully scrutinized for worrying sexual or adult detail. Television was under legal constraints and fairly constant adult scrutiny. Narratives presented could be banal, scary, unsuitable, but they took place only once and usually within organized domestic leisure time. Childhood could be ring-fenced and its texts censored. Now videos can be obtained, owned, enjoyed, replayed again and again by the young child. They can enter fantasy life with a directness and repetition that demands new understandings and new sympathies. How does this consumer-led cultural arte-fact-and-narrative structure affect our children and in what ways does it work?

None of the deep concerns that teachers and educators have about modern consumer culture and the changing nature of childhood can be answered clearly and directly, for none of us can see into the future. We have, however, theoretical tools at our disposal which can be brought to bear on some of the most pervasive dilemmas and yield ways of thinking that throw light on some of the deep knots in the strands of our cultural existence. Feminist thought over the last 20 years has spent time and energy considering questions of gender and the possible reasons for the crude gender stereotypes which the popular culture industry offers us all – even the youngest children.

A CULTURAL INTERPRETATION – GENDER AND POWER

In the teeth of a cultural world which now encompasses a huge range of obvious bodily and sexual difference, artefacts of popular culture such as the tabloid press, romance fiction and women's and men's magazines continuously present us with an essential and opposite dualism of male and female, man and woman. The pervasive assumption of two normative models of development – the heterosexual boy and girl – and the unacknowledged biological determinism which ignores cultural, racial, ethnic, class and historical variation, is viewed by many feminists as a major constituent of repressive sexual politics. These feminists have themselves moved from always opposing and challenging masculine power and bias from an opposite site of difference, one which accepted an essential duality of gender, to one which embraces a more problematic and complex notion of individual sexuality, seeing gender and identity as cultural constructions made up of widely varying personal histories and enactments.[20]

However, many feminists still argue that a particular type of aggressive and assertive masculinity, often associated with male violence and militarism can be seen as a structuring force in maintaining men's power over women and privileging certain patriarchal forms of thought.[21] Others believe that the extreme gendering of many facets of the popular culture industry is a part of a large 'naturalizing' picture that continuously presents and celebrates the female body as men would desire it and simultaneously works to limit the perceived competences of women to the domestic and private sphere. This picture leads eventually to lower expectations of girls in the world of work, to acceptance of lower wages and larger amounts of unpaid domestic work as the 'natural' lot of women compared to men. Thus, the argument runs, that it is often in the interests of capital, certainly of male power, to exclude women from highly paid work and therefore from appropriate aspiration in the public sphere, so that their labour, as housework and childrearing, remains unpaid in the private sphere. Many feminists have written on this subject, delineating the psychological, economic and cultural structures which work together in our language, expectations and family economy to maintain a different positioning of women in society.[22] Many women have succeeded in reshaping these structures, ensuring better opportunities for themselves and the next generation of women. The popular cultural texts about women are also changing, but more slowly than is acknowledged. Men, too, are often unhappy with the powerful 'masculine' roles they are presented with.[23]

So one important cultural and ideological reading of the narratives of the toy industry shows the construction and repetition of a 'hegemonic masculinity' and its corollary: 'emphasized femininity'. Two separate, opposite gender roles are created and maintained through such images and narratives of Superman and Barbie which, by being separate and markedly different, work eventually to hold a hierarchy of male power in place. This concept of 'hegemony' means a social ascendancy achieved in a play of social forces that is not in contests of brute power but lies in the organization of private life and cultural processes. It is not power achieved at the point of a gun, but rather in a set of relationships which is constantly produced in cultural life as 'natural' and legitimate. Other patterns and groups are *subordinated* rather than eliminated. Hegemonic masculinity is constructed in relation both to women and other subordinated masculinities. Emphasized femininity is the necessary support structure of hegemonic masculinity, and is promoted and articulated in mass culture on a vast scale, through toys, stories, women's magazines, romance fiction, television shows, etc., so that central to its maintenance is practice that prevents other models of femininity gaining cultural articulation. As Bob Dixon has pointed out, Barbie's outfits would look extremely silly at a protest march or at Greenham Common, but the veracity of her rigidly expressed femininity is rarely challenged.[24]

However, accepting that hegemonic forces *are* at work in our culture does not mean that a child's school, family, peer group or television texts are *direct* agencies of socialization. That would imply a definite 'script' for any one individual and a complete reception and acceptance of its message. Indeed, close studies of these institutions and their workings show conflicting and contradictory pictures. Schools and families are often in conflict, sometimes within themselves, sometimes with each other and often with larger social structures. In individuals the production of contradictory psychological structures, opposing the practices and philosophies of the surrounding institution and milieu is constantly happening. The post-war theories of mass culture leading to mass thinking and, therefore, to cynical manipulation of the people, have been shown to be inaccurate when people are studied as individuals, as they are then seen actively engaged in making a vast variety of meanings from the cultural material at hand. Ethnographic studies have also shown people working within interpretative communities – groups, families, neighbourhoods – which often vary, sometimes along lines of class, gender, age and ethnicity and sometimes on factors of personality or experience.

In addition to these various receptions and transformations of cultural messages, it is commonly accepted that surface levels of personality are not a straightforward expression of the core of a person's identity. Postmodern thought has shown that one person can embody a variety of subject positions in different areas of their lives and move between them in a playful and active manner. So we must accept that even gender identity is, at some level, unstable, and our model of identity includes matters which lie deep in each individual. As Connell points out:

> A homogeneous or consensual model of gender identity loses the ability to account for creativity and resistance. It recognizes the production of different gender practices only as deviance resulting from inadequate or aberrant socialisation.[25]

However, looking again at the social world around us it is, I believe, possible to see *major patterns of gender behaviour in social practice* alongside minor ones. These are not norms and deviations, rather parts of a whole flux of articulations of different layerings of adult sexuality. But such a postmodern appreciation of the range and variability of gender can, if we are not realistic, prevent us from seeking further understanding and studying the sociological implications of gender positioning and its potentially oppressive features for us and our children. Gender relativism should not prevent us from focusing on deep structures, the discovery and examination of which may yield the key to understanding the culture industry's effects on many children.

A PSYCHOLOGICAL INTERPRETATION: THE UNCONSCIOUS MIND AND GENDERED DESIRES

One important area of theory which throws some light on the complex construction and recognition of masculinity and femininity in our society by proposing and describing a central idea, that of a restless unconscious mind in every individual, is psychoanalysis. This discipline and its discourses address the continual repetitive re-creation of gender stereotypes in our cultural lives, not through examination of large power-based economic structures but through a theory of desire. It attempts to explain why certain formulaic narratives continue to appeal particularly, but not exclusively, to one gender or another over the centuries – romance fiction for women, for example. There are now many psychoanalytic accounts which examine the fictions we create in our culture, and they all bring a theory of individual identity formation to the ways they are constructed and read. Many cultural critics have suggested that the stories we need to hear over and over again are not in place as a result of cultural conditioning but actually respond, sometimes crudely, sometimes imaginatively and beautifully, to a series of deep drives, anxieties and desires which lie in our unconscious minds. Popular culture, because of its width and pervasiveness, can perhaps point most clearly to these desires and how they are satisfied by texts.

According to Freud, the original thinker who first created a whole therapy based around the notion of the unconscious mind, each infant child begins to develop a separate and gendered identity within the common patriarchal structure of the family in Western society through a fateful love of one parent, the mother, which leads to a simultaneous hatred of the other, the father, as a rival. These feelings emerge with the maturing of the child's erotic life between the ages of 4 and 6. With girls the desire for the mother matures into rivalry with her, a desire for a baby and the love of the father, the man who can give her one. This love and need for the male father is eventually transferred onto other men. With boys the mother remains an erotic object, but this desire is repressed by fear of the castrating father, which provokes identification with him and internalization of prohibitions and thus the formation of a strong super-ego. The differing structures of the 'Oedipal crises' for the male and female child are thus the bases of Freudian accounts of the construction of masculinity and femininity.

While his model of the gendered unconscious has been accused of being phallocentric, Eurocentric and ahistorical, Freud first linked the important notions of desire, repression and dreaming, where fantasy life gave rein to erotic impulses which were related to a sense of loss, expressed through unsatisfied desire, all lodged deep in the unconscious. For Freud, through creating stories we express this desire, repeating and working through repressed material: 'desire is inhabited by loss and prohibition, which means it is channelled by rules, including those of language, and subject to forms, including narrative plots.'[26]

Recently and yet similarly, a distinguished feminist psychoanalyst Nancy Chodorow has rewritten this theoretical account of the emergence of sexual identity, also putting object relations in infancy within the typical Western family at the heart of gender construction, but working them out rather differently. Her work perhaps stands at the opposite end of a continuum of thought stretching from Freud. Although there have been many powerful psychoanalytic descriptions of the unconscious mind and the ways fictions work to express desire, it is perhaps fruitful to consider the similarities, 50 years later, between her account and that of Freud. In *The Reproduction of Mothering*, Chodorow argues that the girl child's intense love of the mother usually grows into identification with her and that this love is integrated into adult subjectivity as she matures. There is, however, a break and separation for boys as they grow into men. The necessary overcoming of the intense infant-mother love often results in a manifestly violent break with the mother as independent masculinity is established.[27]

Thus, both Freud and Chodorow attempt to identify and describe a 'typical' and recurring pattern of sexuality and desire. Like all psychoanalytic accounts, theirs point to a deep sense of loss which they claim all humans suffer as individual identity is established, as each child begins to discover that he or she is a separate being. In both their accounts this loss is worked out in terms of desire (which is created by the need to come to terms with loss), differently for boys and girls. Each set of desires yields different fantasies for the different genders as independent gendered identity is established. There is no doubt that if we consider the plot structure of many 'typical' fictions residing in popular culture many of them do appear to resonate with essential features of these psychoanalytic accounts. Looking, for example, at the current toy catalogues, with their highly gendered narratives of princess fashion dolls and baby dolls to care for as mothers for little girls and pages of warrior figures with mutant enemies and technological weapons for little boys, these popular images and narratives suggest differing and powerful inner desires and fantasies for both sexes, clumsily and variously expressed, but with constant and reiterating patterns. The little girls' toys and stories point to a strong fantasy identification with the mother role, which is what many little girls *appear to desire* together with a need to attract the male gaze, an almost narcissistic obsession with making themselves into objects of beauty. Here psychoanalytic theory would point to a female pattern of loss and desire: identification and rivalry with the mother and simultaneous desire for, and a need to attract the (repressed) male father. Similarly, the little boys' toys speak of aggression, of narratives of violence against the body, particularly the female body, and this again often *seems to chime with their growing internal organization of masculine subjectivity.* The boys, the theory suggests, desire to establish their separate masculine identity through a fantasy of violence against the (repressed) mother.

How stable, how accurate and again how useful are these theories of the unconscious? Both Freud and Chodorow recognized that no one pattern of development can be taken as fixed or universal. So their theories are suggestive of pattern, not reductive or stable. What psychoanalytic theory presents us with is the idea that the *unconscious mind* plays an important role in the development of gendered identity and that that identity is continually being created and changed throughout a person's life history, so that masculinity and femininity are normally internally fissured and in tension. Also in psychoanalytic theory the kind of explanation of an individual's behaviour is inherently a narrative one itself: it claims an enhanced understanding of the present through histories of the past that have been blocked from consciousness, and therefore it contains the possibility of change. But most importantly it suggests that desire is often gendered in the particularities of the differing fantasies of the male and female and that this fantasy material is a powerful force in the structuring of our stories and our literature. We are by nature, it suggests, fiction making beings, and so the power of popular fictions is that they constantly address the desires and conflicts of sexual identity.

The idea that gender and genre are related in our culture has been pointed out by several scholars, showing how, although historically unstable, with forms and ideas that change over time, there is a strong case to be made that over the last two hundred years certain forms of writing, certain genres that appear to attract gendered understanding and desire have stabilized within popular culture.[28] Adventure stories have been fairly consistently written for men, with a male hero who has a primary relationship with a male villain; love stories have been written and received by a consistent female readership, each one with a female heroine whose primary relationship is with a male hero.[29] Putting these pervasive genres down beside psychoanalytic theory and the latest toy catalogues, it is possible to see fertile connections which might help us to understand children's growing sexuality and its relationship to their developing literacy practices. It is interesting to speculate, for example, how often the villains, for boys, have *female characteristics and powers* which derive from mutant or alien sources. Resonances of repressed anxieties of violent separation and hatred of the female mother seem to run through the peculiarities of the villains in the male adventure story. So, in boys' adventure stories, often *the villain is feminized*: smooth, hairless, plump and softly spoken, like the Joker in *Batman* or the cat-stroking unseen villain, head of SMERSH in James Bond movies: always contrasting with the clean-cut, muscular and 'straight' masculinity of the hero. With a similar psychoanalytic reading it is noticeable that the desired male figure in female romances is often strong, reliable, *fatherly*. In two of the latest Disney narratives for girls, *The Little Mermaid* and *Pocahontas*, the mother has been removed altogether and the heroine plays out a 'Freudian' narrative of love of the father being challenged and then restored by the love of an equally strong and competent young hero.

THE DEEP PLAY OF NARRATIVE FANTASY

Returning to playing children and their narrative fantasies, if we accept a role for the unconscious, it makes sense that certain powerful magical fantasies, replayed again and again, allow children to organize and express their identities in certain kinds of necessary and pleasurable ways. Viewing the unconscious as a source of a series of erotic impulses and desires, which have to be repressed but which continuously challenge their somewhat precarious structure of identity in the social world and cannot therefore be directly expressed in consciousness, it also makes sense that children, like adults, *need to fantasize*, to dream. Popular fictions seem often shamelessly to address and repeat the dream themes which allow the pleasure of organizing growing sexual identity, with its intense anxieties and repressed material. Children's continuous repetition of highly gendered play narratives, from Power Rangers to Barbie, are perhaps a way of repeating to themselves fantasies of potent desire.

This attempt to link the insights of psychoanalytic theory with the plot structure of much gendered popular narrative fantasy can point not only to how and why many children play with toy figures, but also to how they might be moved from this primitive and private level of narration to one where their developing imaginative powers can consider and recast the cultural material at hand. None of these accounts are reductive, and we often find evidence of children doing totally different things with toys and narratives. There are other desires lying in the unconscious: dreams of power for warrior girls, dreams of domestic love and affection for boys. In addition to organizing and testing their adult sexual identities, children are also engaged in dreams of other adult competences. Literature for children, with its rich cultural references, often works with a dream of child power, where children are the main protagonists and the adults are banished or incompetent. Here again it is by focusing intently on the plot structures of popular books and stories, seeing patterns and repetitions, that we are able to understand the grain of desire that lies in these narrative texts. The books of Roald Dahl, such as *George's Marvellous Medicine*, often yield triumphant and vicious satisfaction of the reversal of power in child over adult. The much-loved *Famous Five* series by Enid Blyton speaks directly of a display of child competence over the bumbling, stupid and often criminal behaviour of adults. However, the final link in this chain of argument which helps link the popular to literature is that narratives for children and adults are often pleasurable and primitive not only because they address and temporarily ease inner conflicts, but also because they work according to rules.

THE STRUCTURES OF NARRATIVE DESIRE

Understanding the rules of narrative desire, seeing how they work in popular fictions and building on them in the classroom is, then, at the heart of the literacy curriculum if we wish to connect children with literature. The beginning of a story can set up a tingling of unsatisfied but expectant pleasure because we know the rules, and they will not let us down. With a good story the beginning hooks us and the end leaves a feeling of satiation but also an instinct to repeat the experience again and again. But, often more importantly, between the beginning and the end is the delightful dilatory space, the twists and turns of plot, the luxury of sub-plots and immersion in the detail of context.[30] Here, children can begin to try other subject positions, leaving total identification with the main protagonist to one side, to play with delay, topsy-turveys, linguistic games, to notice or create advances and retreats, always knowing the end will, must, yield total and triumphant satisfaction. This dilatory space is one which children inhabit when they play with toys. The beginnings and ends of the story have been established: the superhero has conquered, the princess has won her man, the little pony has returned home and been put to bed; ends have served out their wonderful, predictable measure of pleasure. But children, like adults, want to sustain that pleasure, to return again and again to the dilatory space in the grand narrative as *agents and authors* of their own satisfaction, taking risks, deferring gratification. This is what the toy industry knows so well, its figures offering an enticing invitation to enter the pleasurable, autonomous dilatory space in a familiar narrative.

In their famous analyses of folktales, the Russian formalists made a distinction between the plot or *sjuzet*, which is the underlying structure of narrative, a tension which drives it forward through time and makes it into what we recognize as a story, and the wealth and meaningfulness of contextual detail

in which the story is embedded, the *fabula*. We have seen how
a narrative text provides a desirable plot, one which in popular
fictions often seems to chime with psychoanalytic accounts of
differing desires associated with the constructing of gendered
identity by young readers, but these are also played out in an
important world of reference. It is here, in the distinction
between the *sjuzet* and the *fabula*, that we can bring a sympath-
etic understanding of deep desire lodged in the unconscious, a
psychoanalytic 'reading' of many popular fictions and images,
to the possibilities of cultural and enriching change in the contextual detail, to the *fabula:* the settings and language of stories.
Watching and listening to her 4-year-olds' highly gendered play
narratives in the nursery, Vivian Gussin Paley[31] noted again and
again not only the different plots of the boys' and girls' stories
(the boys constantly fantasizing superhero dramas of violence
and destruction, the girls busily and messily creating fantasies
of family life in the doll corner), but also the widely different
contextual detail used and enjoyed by the different fantasies.
Only once did she manage to read a book that was enjoyed by
all: *The Boxcar Children* by Gertrude Chandler Warner, and for a
short while the boys enjoyed the homey pleasures of the doll
corner. 'The happy ending is superfluous . . . The class,' she
points out, 'is interested only in the house in the woods, and
continually repeats the act of making a boxcar into a home . . .
The essential element is self-reliance.' Here again is evidence
that play often occupies this dilatory space between beginnings
and ends, and that *it is the detail of the fabula* in which children,
like all readers, invest considerable desire. When I read Blyton's
Five Go Off to Camp as a child, it was the details of camping
that I found so fascinating, setting up tiny camps in my bedroom
and playing out other narratives. Here there is a direct link with
cultural topic work in the primary school. Working with popular
stories and literature can enrich the *fabula* of the children's
stories, if teachers understand and adapt them to incorporate
pleasurable narratives. Topics from the history curriculum, such
as the Ancient Greeks or the Second World War, can be stagger-
ingly successful if stories are incorporated into the heart of
meaning making, stories which respect gendered fantasy and
yet work to enrich its *fabula*. For many children the details of
history and geography cohere around narratives.

Looking again at the playing child, we can see a deep level

of personal fantasy being enacted. Theories of narrative desire can help us understand in ways that can embellish, elaborate and enrich those stories. Understanding and sympathizing with the pleasures of such play, taking note of children's growing sexual organization, can help us sensitively to unlock further texts. Working with the grain of desire helps us introduce children to literature which eventually opens out more possibilities, more various responses. What we don't have to accept, and nor do our children, is the particular narrow, consumerist, temporary and deadly cultural *fabula* in which many popular culture narratives are set. A model of literacy teaching that works with growing consciousness can build on the products and freedoms of the popular culture industry, not closing the classroom door on gendered fantasies and indulging in moral panic. Re-enactments of triumphant and pleasurable masculinities and femininities are presented in literature, in myth and legend to feed the appetites of even the youngest children. It is by ring-fencing our children in an idealized, ungendered childish world, ignoring material which might address their growing adult *gendered* subjectivities, that we allow them to become bored with literacy. Classrooms rich with popular stories, narrative topic work and possibilities for play are places which, through respecting desire in children, can help them both luxuriate in pleasure and eventually transform for themselves the cultural messages embodied in plastic figures.

NOTES

1 E. Guhl and W. Koner, *The Greeks and Romans: Their Life and Customs*, London: Bracken Books, 1989.
2 Jerome Bruner, *Actual Minds, Possible Worlds*, Cambridge, Mass.: Harvard University Press, 1986.
3 Jerome L. Singer, 'Imaginative Play and Adaptive Development', in Jeffrey Goldstein (ed.), *Toys, Play and Child Development*, Cambridge: Cambridge University Press, 1994.
4 Vivien Gussin Paley, *Walley's Stories: Conversations in the Kindergarten*, Cambridge, Mass.: Harvard University Press, 1981, p. 29.
5 Many native animals were actually considered by the adult world as vermin. Rabbits were being shot and eaten in many households where *Peter Rabbit* was read in the nursery.
6 Kimberly Reynolds, *Children's Literature in the 1890s and the 1990s*, Plymouth: Northcote House, 1994.

7 Carolyn Steedman, *Strange Dislocations: Childhood and the Idea of Human Interiority 1780–1930*, London: Virago, 1995.

8 Marina Warner, *Managing Monsters: Six Myths of our Time, The Reith Lectures*, London: Vintage, 1994, p. 41.

9 Richard deCordova, 'The Mickey in Macy's Window', in E. Smoodin (ed.), *Disney Discourse: Producing the Magic Kingdom*, New York and London: Routledge, 1994, p. 203.

10 deCordova, op. cit., p. 204.

11 Greg S. McCue with Clive Bloom, *Dark Knights: The New Comics in Context*, London and Colorado: Pluto, 1993, pp. 19, 6.

12 Gussin Paley, op. cit., p. 129.

13 Mark Cotta Vaz, *Tales of the Dark Night*, New York: Balantine Books, 1989, p. 31, quoted in McCue with Bloom, op. cit., p. 23.

14 McCue with Bloom, op. cit.

15 *The Toy Industry in the United Kingdom 1992*, London: British Toy and Hobby Association, 1992.

16 Douglas Gomery, 'Disney's Business History', in Smoodin, op. cit.

17 Bob Dixon, *Playing Them False: A Study of Children's Toys, Games and Puzzles*, Stoke-on-Trent: Trentham, 1990.

18 Brian Sutton-Smith, 'Does Play Prepare the Future?', in Goldstein, op. cit.

19 *Annual Report of British Toys and Hobby Industry*, London: 1994.

20 Gisela Bock and Susan James (eds), *Beyond Equality and Difference: Citizenship, Feminine Politics and Female Subjectivity*, London: Routledge, 1992.

21 Miriam Cooke and Angela Woollacott (eds), *Gendering War Talk*, Princeton, N.J.: Princeton University Press, 1993.

22 There is a considerable body of feminist writing on these subjects. Two important texts are Carole Gillingham, *In a Different Voice: Psychological Theory and Women's Development*, Harvard, Mass.: Harvard University Press, 1982; Sylvia Walby, *Theorizing Patriarchy*, Oxford: Blackwell, 1990.

23 Jeff Hearn and D. Morgan (eds), *Men, Masculinities and Social Theory*, London: Unwin Hyman, 1990.

24 Dixon, op. cit.

25 R. W. Connell, *Gender and Power*, Cambridge: Polity Press, 1987, p. 194.

26 Peter Brooks, *Psychoanalysis and Storytelling: The Bucknell Lectures in Literary Theory*, Oxford: Blackwell, 1994, p. 25.

27 Nancy Chodorow, *The Reproduction of Mothering*, Berkeley, Calif.: University of California Press, 1978.

28 To me the two most powerful books that I have read on this subject are Graham Dawson, *Soldier Heroes: British Adventure, Empire and the Imagining of Masculinities*, London: Routledge, 1994; Janice A. Radway, *Reading the Romance: Women, Patriarchy and Popular Literature*, London: Verso, 1984.

29 John. G. Cawelti, *Adventure, Mystery and Romance*, Chicago: University of Chicago Press, 1976.

30 These ideas are more fully developed in Peter Brooks, *Reading for*

the Plot: Design and Intention in Narrative, Oxford: Clarendon Press, 1984, Chapter 4.

31 Vivien Gussin Paley, *Boys and Girls: Superheroes in the Doll Corner*, Chicago: University of Chicago Press, 1984.

FURTHER READING

In addition to the works cited I would suggest the following:

Barrs, M. and Pigeon, S. (eds), *Reading the Difference: Gender and Reading in the Primary School*, London: Centre for Language in Primary Education (CLPE), 1993.

Bettelheim, Bruno, *The Uses of Enchantment: The Meaning and Importance of Fairy Tales*, London: Penguin, 1991.

Chodorow, Nancy J., *Femininities, Masculinities, Sexualities: Freud and Beyond*, London: Free Association Books, 1994.

Radford, Jean (ed.), *The Progress of Romance: The Politics of Popular Fiction*, London: Routledge & Kegan Paul, 1986.

Styles, Morag, Bearne, Eve and Watson, Victor (eds), *After Alice: Exploring Children's Literature*, London: Cassell, 1992.

Styles, Morag, Bearne, Eve and Watson, Victor (eds), *The Prose and the Passion: Children and Their Reading*, London: Cassell, 1994.

Chapter 2

Reality in boxes
Children's perception of television narratives

David Whitley

My mother groaned, my father wept –
Into the dangerous world I leapt,
Helpless, naked, piping loud,
Like a fiend hid in a cloud.
      (William Blake, *Infant Sorrow*)

INTO THE DANGEROUS WORLD

Perhaps, as adults, we all have more of an investment than we care to realize in children's innocence. Certainly, as my own children grow up and the focus of their television viewing begins to shift from the safe nurturing havens of *Spot, Postman Pat* and the excellent *Pingu* towards the relatively wilder shores of *Batman* and *Power Rangers* I am aware of some anxiety, a sense of loss even. That anxiety is heightened by the knowledge that *Batman* and *Power Rangers* are themselves sites of innocence in comparison to many of the images and genres my children are going to encounter later on. Projecting forwards, it is possible to become involved in a gut-wrenching spin in which one's children are seen as constantly vulnerable – potential victims at all times to unsafe streets, violent films and computer pornography.

In the context of such persistent and corrosive exposure, the sense of loss of a relatively safe childhood becomes almost unbearable. It is easy to forget that the ways in which we experience the world have always been fraught with danger, that as adults we have nearly all reached our own – in some cases uneasy – accommodation of them. It is easy to forget that the range of unpleasant, startling, absorbing or merely boring images I have experienced on the screen myself over the years has enabled me to become relatively clear about what I like and what I need from television in order to feel informed, alive to the world and its possibilities.

Children, of course, are particularly vulnerable but are also more resilient than we sometimes allow. As adults, we are anxious about the children we care for, partly because so much of what they learn from television seems to take place independently of our wishes, aspirations and control. Most adults know little in detail about what their children watch on television, at least after they reach school age. Parents and teachers (even those researching the area!) know even less about how they respond. The reflections that follow, then, are, of necessity, formed from a shared perspective of relative ignorance and a shared wish to know more.

THE CLASSROOM AGENDA

A scene you could reproduce in a hundred different ways in thousands of classrooms up and down the country. I'm working with a year 5 class of 9- and 10-year-olds, using a particular literary genre as a focus to explore a variety of issues. In this case our starting point is *Aesop's Fables*, but it could be anything – fairy-tale, adventure, contemporary fiction, poem. We work towards a project in which the children will write 'fables' of their own, with the constraints of the genre fairly freely interpreted and an opportunity offered to illustrate as well as write the text they produce. Later, we will gather their illustrated tales into a book of class stories. The results, of course, are very varied, even though nearly all the children put considerable care and effort into their work. One boy expends endless effort on reproducing the precise contours of Sonic the Hedgehog (is Sonic a descendant of the fable tradition?), the character from Sega's computer game series whose antics, I assume, absorb much of his time and attention at home. There is a rather clever pastiche of detective fiction – a deliberate parody come homage to the popular *Inspector Morse* series in which the eponymous Morse becomes Mouse. Another child relates a brief tale of animal one-upmanship – a prevalent theme in the classical fable tradition – in which the illustration dominates the text. The narrative has absorbed many of the linguistic features of cartoon – from 'Na, na!' to 'Kersplat!' as the overconfident animal gets its violent comeuppance. Others – mostly girls – use the format to explore a range of serious issues, with varying degrees of subtlety and control in the way they develop their narratives.

I am not their regular class teacher. For me this is a 'research' project and I am more interested in the full range of modes through which the literary genre has been interpreted than in making value judgements on the results. And, inevitably, in a modern classroom where children are offered a fairly open format to produce narrative writing, a great variety of media sub-texts permeate their accounts. But – inevitably also in a classroom context – the most interesting writing (the 'richest', as we say) from the viewpoint of a class teacher, is that which has a strong literary dimension, its media-inspired themes successfully subordinated to the demands of a more literary development. The classroom is dominated, overtly and in terms of unexamined assumptions, by a literary curriculum and, despite many teachers' honourable attempts to extend beyond these terms of reference, children will eventually be judged in terms of criteria which are almost exclusively literary.

I want, of course, to value the painstaking work of the boy who spends all his time producing as exact as possible a copy of his favourite *Sonic the Hedgehog* image: the cartoon-inspired narratives of birds getting their 'ya-boo-sucks' comeuppance. But unless these children can use their media-inspired sources to generate work that fulfils more literary requirements, in the terms within which schools assess their language-based development, they are doomed to failure. And they are likely to be perceived by teachers as examples of young writers whose potential creativity has been stunted, rather than stimulated, by an experience of media narrative that will seem to adults to have acted like a fix – a drug arresting development.

Polarizing literary and media texts in this way fails to recognize very extensive areas of overlap and cross-influence. A majority, perhaps, of media narratives could be traced back in terms of origins or influence to literary genres, and much television and film, especially where it has acquired a 'classic' status, is valued in overtly literary terms. But holding the two categories apart like this does enable one to see more clearly where the problem lies. For, as teachers, we inherit a discourse for discriminating literary value which is centuries old, extraordinarily rich and varied. By contrast, the distinctive language that has been developed for discussing media texts is relatively recent, often draws on a specialist, offputtingly technical vocabulary and has generally focused on the function, rather than value, of the texts described. Thus, where media texts have been valued this has tended to be within the terms of the older literary language; where they have been perceived merely as 'popular', they have been subjected to semiotic and cultural analysis but, in so far as they resist a literary appropriation, have continued to be seen as essentially low-grade or even corruptive. At one end of the spectrum, computer games, with their repetitive, violent plots, can yield rich results for semiotic or cultural analysis. But, though you might notice analogies to the battle scenes of stories from the epic tradition (which also tend to draw on a repetitive formula), you would be hard pressed to defend them as worthy descendants from Homer. At the other end of the spectrum, TV series like *Inspector Morse*, with its rich interweavings of literary reference and themes, *Blackadder* and dramatizations of classic stories are readily appreciated for qualities such as subtlety, complexity or wit that have long currency in literary discourse.

There are, I think, two related problems for work in the classroom here. First, the difficulty of finding an accessible language within which media texts can be valued means that those texts which are used in the classroom are likely to be viewed in predominantly literary terms. That is, we miss out on discussing the way they function distinctively as media texts, focusing only on their literary dimensions. As a correlative to this, and perhaps more damagingly, media texts without any obvious literary quality are unlikely to gain any serious attention in the classroom in their own right. At best, they may be introduced as adjuncts to work of literary value – relationships between characters on soaps as a lead-in to considering tensions between characters in Shakespeare's plays, and so on. Generally, media texts are likely to be crowded out of an already overpacked curriculum or to be seen as impeding the development of literary quality in children's writing.

There is, then, it seems to me, a need for a critical vocabulary that will enable us to perceive the distinctive qualities of media texts more clearly and usefully. The acid test for such a vocabulary is that it should atune us, as adults, to what children are saying about the ways in which they already value and use media texts. Their words should become more meaningful to us. In the process it may be possible to take on board the understanding they are developing of media texts as a more positive part of our account of their learning generally. Much of the work that has gone on in media education over recent years has, of course, been seeking to promote both a theoretical framework and set of classroom practices designed to move us in precisely this direction. My point here is not that this extremely important work needs to be superseded, but that certain key elements in it may need to be emphasized more clearly. Most centrally, in conceptual terms, we need to understand much more about a range of issues embedded in the term 'modality'.

REALITY MOVES

The term 'modality' was brought into media studies from linguistics. It is used to discriminate the degree to which we attribute reality to any given statement or related sequence of events. As such, it is related, it seems to me (though I have not found this point made in the literature on the subject), to the central project with which literary criticism has traditionally involved itself. Aristotle defined the project of literature as *mimesis* – different forms of imitation of reality. And literary criticism has, at least until very recently, concerned itself predominantly with discriminating and assessing the different kinds of reality effect produced within literary forms. This is as pervasive in the most sophisticated forms of analysis – evaluating the form of Shakespeare's sonnets in relation to shifting economic and social structures in Elizabethan England, and so on – as it is in the criteria used in assessing the most basic forms of children's writing. What teachers look for in a child's account of their summer holiday – alongside fluency and grammatical competence – are qualities such as vividness and particularity that 'bring the story to life', which serve to enhance its reality effect. The mimetic tradition, in all its various forms, is so deeply instilled in most teachers' thinking about writing, and narrative in particular, that we are generally hardly conscious of it as a specific conceptual framework.

But if the discourse of literary criticism offers a vocabulary honed, over centuries of use, to explore the most precise nuances and farreaching implications of 'reality effects' within writing, why do we need another concept to describe the same thing? Especially as 'modality' does not exactly trip easily off the tongue? To answer this it may be useful to look in more detail at what is involved in the concept of modality.

The best starting point for defining the concept of modality is its use in language; it was within linguistics that the term was originally developed. In English we have a wide variety of verbs which we call 'modal auxiliaries'. These modify the function of the verb to which they are attached and, in so doing, alter the modality of the sentence. We could, for instance, alter the modality of the sentence '*There is a man on the stairs*' by substituting the modal auxiliary verb '*might*' for '*is*': '*There might be a man on the stairs*'. Here, the degree of reality we are likely to ascribe to the situation defined in the sentence is much diminished by the addition of the modal auxiliary. The man's presence on the stairs is now only a possibility: the modality of the sentence has been weakened.

It is not only the verb which defines modality, however. Negation, for instance, also modifies modality, often in complex and potentially unstable ways. The sentence '*There is not a man on the stairs*' does not simply cancel the statement '*There is a man on the stairs*', asserting an equally strong modality in the reverse direction. To state that there is not a man on the stairs is to assume that there might have been a man there. The degree to which this may further modify the modality of the statement is dependent on the context within which the statement is made and received. A person who had recently been attacked by a man might attribute a very different modality to the statement '*There is not a man on the stairs*', for instance, compared to someone who had no reason to feel threatened. Likewise, the statement made at night near an unlit stairwell would be likely to have a more intense modal operation than if uttered in daylight on a crowded shopping mall. Modality, then, is not fixed by the form of an utterance. It can vary with context, and indeed with the attitude and perceptual skew of the hearer.

If this rudimentary sketch has clarified some of the functions of modality within linguistics, it should now be possible to consider more fully its application to media studies. In our discussion of modality in relation to sentences we began with the function of verbs. Film sequences, as we now know, like sentences, have a particular kind of grammar which enables them to be read coherently. As with language, viewers become conversant with the rules by which this grammar operates through their repeated exposure to the medium. Although the analogy is not exact, there are some similarities between the functions of verbs in sentences and the use of the 'cut' in film sequences. Like a verb, a cut can change the tense of a given sequence of events: a flashback puts us into the past tense, change to another location may develop a parallel present, a cut may move us ahead in time, and so on. As experienced viewers, we rarely make mistakes in reading such cuts accurately, as they indicate the relationship of events to the time sequences of the whole narrative development, but the process is a complex one, often involving a number of visual, aural and verbal cues that need to be assimilated if the correct judgement is to be made. And film makers often exploit areas of ambiguity in the ensuing modality judgements audiences are led to make about the sequences they are watching. Thrillers and horror films, in particular, regularly exploit the potential instability of such judgements, leading us into dream sequences as if they were reality or future time etc. in order to shock us. In a sense this deliberate *play* with the audience's modality judgements becomes part of the aesthetic of the genre and needs to be taken account of as we try to understand why people appear to derive pleasure from watching events that are horrific or frightening. For it is a shared understanding of play that allows audiences to enjoy being manipulated into states of confusion and fear which, as individuals, they would in other contexts find intolerable.

There is a paradox here, which is wider in its application than any particular genre of media narrative, though. This stems from the more general notion that, although television particularly would seem to offer the potential for an extremely high degree of modality, since the camera records what is directly in front of it and 'cannot lie', as they say, many genres of television production, especially those for younger children, in fact assert very weak modality. The cartoon, whether serialized in children's comics or animated for film and television production, is the prime example of this phenomenon. Within this form a whole series of auditory and visual cues, from highly stylized voices to one-dimensional forms and caricatured features, register the unreality of the medium. It is indeed this degree of unreality, the weak modality expectations built into the whole genre, which allows actions that would have grotesque, gruesome or tragic outcomes if played out in more realistic formats to be perceived as funny or entertaining. Children would hardly be entertained by the violent depradations enacted every few seconds on the protagonists' bodies in *Tom and Jerry* cartoons and the like if they felt the characters to be in any way real. This instance has been deployed as a very effective line of argument against those who see a direct causal link between the *quantity* of violence children are exposed to through television narratives and unacceptable levels of violence within society. But, though the point is well taken, we still understand too little about children's emotional and cognitive reactions to narratives to settle many of the more complex issues involved with confidence. What is clear, though, is that modality judgements are crucial in determining response to narratives of all kinds, and that perception of media narratives, in particular, can be drastically changed by the degree to which events related are seen to be carrying high or weak modality. Adults worried about children's exposure to cartoons, who focus solely on the *content* of narratives containing persistent scenes of violence, fail to account for the most striking feature determining children's overtly pleasurable response: the perceived unreality of the form. In so doing, they also fail to listen to what children can tell us about the way they understand and respond to events in film narratives. This is strikingly clear in relation to cartoons, where the form transforms the manifest content into an occasion for pleasurable excitement and laughter. But a similar process takes place, in more subtle ways, in relation to other forms, too, where an adult view based largely on response to the content of the narrative fails to account sufficiently for the way children's perception of modality affects their engagement with the events depicted. I shall explore this notion in more detail towards the end of this chapter, but I would like to turn first to a specific example of ways in which more subtle kinds of play with modality judgements within film narrative may be perceived by children.

CHILDREN FRAMING RESPONSE

The sequence I want to focus on occurs towards the end of Walt Disney's animated version of *The Jungle Book*, which was released fairly recently on video, nearly 30 years after it was first produced as a film. Disney's overwhelming domination of the market in children's feature-length video cartoons has been the result of a marketing strategy to stimulate demand by releasing a number of their classic film animations on video format alongside a new wave of more recent feature-length productions. These films, often watched repeatedly, have now begun to form a major strand of young children's viewing experience.

The sequence I wish to focus on involves the resolution of the main line of dramatic tension in the story – the threat of the tiger Shere Khan on the life of the young 'man cub' Mowgli that has been the underlying impetus for most of the film's action. When the tiger finally encounters the young boy, Mowgli faces up to him with undaunted, though naive, courage and has to be rescued by his boon companion and surrogate father, Baloo the bear. In the ensuing battle, Baloo appears to be killed and the film leads the viewer's emotions, through identification with Mowgli, rapidly from exultation through to grief at the big-hearted bear's death. This emotional climax is extended, deepened – and later reprised – by means of a funeral oration attributing heroic grandeur to Baloo's act of self-sacrifice and spoken largely off camera by the panther Bagheera. The audience focuses on Baloo's big, splayed inert body while Bagheera winds up his elegiac oration so that we witness the bear's coming to consciousness, as one eye opens, while the other characters, unaware, are absorbed in grief and rhetorical outpourings. Thus, elegy turns to mock elegy, grief and grandeur receive their ironic counterpoint in Baloo's appreciation of the eloquence of Bagheera's speech, and tragedy, finally, turns back into comedy.

This is an adult's 'reading', couched deliberately in literary terms of analysis, of this scene. But what do children make of it? To what extent is such a literary framework for analysis appropriate in trying to understand their response? To begin to address some of the issues contained in these questions I have turned, first, to my own children who, by the time I began questioning them in detail, must have watched the film around a dozen times. Jack, in particular, used to watch the film spell-bound, his eyes glazed and an obvious lump in his throat each time he witnessed the scene of Baloo's apparent death towards the end. Yet I knew also, from remarks the children made after they had watched *Bambi* a couple of times, that strong emotional response and obvious fascination with the story did not necessarily mean that they had understood the significance of details which adults would think fundamental to the plot. I wanted to understand more of what form their understanding and response took. Here are some extracts of my recorded conversations with them:

Myself: But what was frightening about Shere Khan, do you think?

Jack: He had claws?

Eve: No, no, Mowgli *was* frightened.

Jack: . . . claws were sharp, as big as that [*demonstrates*].

Self: They were long weren't they? Yeah. What did he do with the claws – do you remember?

Jack: Yeah. He killed Baloo.

Self: He killed Baloo.

Jack: He wasn't really. He doesn't know that because of the fire – frightened him off. . . .

Self: That's very good. Do you think Shere Khan was a real tiger?

Jack: No, no.

Self: Why don't you think he was a real tiger?

Jack: 'Cos he's just in the television.

Self: He's just in the television, right. And what . . . would he have looked different if he was a real tiger?

Jack: He he would . . . would he . . . he would, mmm, have been made by God.

Self: Right. Who made him in the television, do you think?

Jack: Mmm – some people.

Self: Hmmm. And how do you think they would have made him?

Jack: 'Cos I – 'cos once I had a look at the television and people made him.

Self: People made him, did they?

Jack: Hmmm – so that's not a real tiger.

  . . .

Jack: Nobody is real.
Self: Nobody is real.
Jack: 'Cos they drawed them.

My son was 5 years old when I had this conversation with him. Eve, who clarifies an earlier point in dispute by insisting that Mowgli *was* frightened at the start of the extract, was nearly 4. For me the most striking thing about what the children say here is that, although they had been emotionally very affected by this scene – they had each watched it entranced many times, often with eyes glazed and an obvious lump in the throat – Jack appears very comfortable with the idea that it is not 'real'. He is obviously conscious of its weak modality – all the characters are unreal as people have 'drawed them' – and indeed is very clear about the producedness of the text (as we say!); but this seems rather to interest than to bother him. Nor does it appear to conflict with his continuing to have a very powerful emotional response as he views it.

But to what extent does his emotional response and under-standing mesh with the literary framework for interpreting this scene which I sketched earlier? Let me first develop this rudi-mentary sketch a little further by suggesting that there are at least three possible levels of response to the scene, each of increasing complexity. I will call these the *emotive*, the *ironic* and the *aesthetic* dimensions of response, although I recognize that they cannot really be separated so neatly as this. The emotive response calls forth our raw feelings – largely fear, excitement and loss – and our empathetic engagement with the narrative process leading us from relief to grief and then through to restored joy. The ironic level includes these emotive responses but partakes of the intellectual pleasure that is generated through the irony of our knowing that Baloo is alive while Bagheera is still in the process of completing his elegy. The aesthetic level of response is dependent on each of the others but includes awareness of the text as artfully produced in order to generate these responses. This awareness includes the poten-tial to become critical – as well as appreciative. The levels could be represented like this:

EMOTIVE	Grief → Joy
	(Tragedy → Comedy)
IRONIC	Elegy → Celebration
	(Mock Elegy)
AESTHETIC	Awareness of ways in which these effects produced. Reflexive consciousness.

If I change the terms of reference of this scheme a little, I could say that this film's aesthetic depends, as did the examples from the horror genre alluded to earlier, on the audience's participating in a deliberate play with modality judgement at a crucial point in the narrative. We have to allow ourselves to be taken in, that is, by the assertion of Baloo's apparent death in order to become fully emotionally involved in the scene – then we use our awareness of the ways in which we have been taken in to gain full aesthetic pleasure. But is this scheme helpful in identifying levels of response – and development – in children? Some further extracts from conversation with my son suggest, I would argue, that it may be:

Self: Yeah. And did Baloo die in the end do you think?
Jack: No, he didn't.
Self: What happened to him when he was on the ground then?
Jack: He was dead – dead doesn't mean died.
Self: It doesn't?

. . .

Self: Why do you think Mowgli and Bagheera thought he was dead then?
Jack: Because they're only just drawn and they don't think as much as us.

Watching the whole film with Jack on several occasions prior to this conversation it was clear that the power it had for him derived in the first instance from the emotional response he had, which was very strong. But here, though I have perhaps led him to some extent through my questions, one could interpret his statements as indicating that he is on the edge of being able to respond to the sequence at other levels too. 'Dead doesn't mean died': is he simply confused here? Or is he struggling to put into words something of the complex, contradictory process we are asked to engage in as we change our assessment of the modality of the film's central assertion of the 'death' of Baloo? Jack has already come to some of the understanding he would need to move to an aesthetic response to the sequence: he knows something about the producedness of the form he is watching. But an aesthetic response is dependent on recognizing the way ironies are played out in the sequence too, and this, in turn, is dependent on our awareness that the precepts on which some of the characters in the film are acting are partial, indeed flawed.

Jack is, of course, much too young to understand the concept of irony. But is his statement that Bagheera and Mowgli are only drawn – 'they don't think as much as us' – a way of recognizing that these characters display a limited – in fact, false – awareness of what is going on at this point in the film? Is being able to say 'they don't think as much as us' a route towards understanding that they don't know as much as us, at this stage, because they have not, with us, been able to witness Baloo's eyes open, to hear him speak? I do not know that this is the case, though it must surely be a possibility. If it is so, then he may be edging towards a sense of the central irony that is in play here. What this makes very clear, though, is that children's understanding is developed and stretched by making the kinds of – often confused – modality judgements that these statements bear witness to. As a good friend of mine is apt to remind me, confusion can be a form of theorizing.

The advantage of running the concept of modality alongside a more traditional literary assessment of what is going on in this scene is that it allows us to become more positively interested in the stages through which such confusions take us. In the process, it should also enable us to think more clearly and specifically about the media dimensions of what is being viewed. Though this may be seen as a sequence of literary value, it matters that the images are hand-drawn cartoons, that the effect of irony is *produced* through the restricted viewpoint which the frame of the screen creates. It may also matter that this was originally produced as a film nearly 30 years ago, that the long period of gestation before its appearance now on video is the result of the hugely influential Disney Corporation's marketing strategy. And, of course, it may matter that it derives from a narrative written for children by Rudyard Kipling, at a high point of British colonial expansion; that the film was produced in the late 1960s as America was trying to absorb the counter-cultural challenge to the work ethic; and that the video has been released late in our post-colonial history, with the voice of the Anglicized Indian Mowgli deeply inflected in the language and intonations of mid-century (though now seemingly universalized!) America. For all its appeal and apparent univer-sality, the struggle for survival between boy and tiger is not culturally innocent. The film's modality – its 'reality effect' – is constructed by children and adults alike, actively engaged in the process of viewing, and may draw on awareness of its producedness that derives from any or all of these perspectives. Critical awareness – the way we interpret and relate to the film's reality effect and the value we ascribe to it – will be shaped and articulated differently according to the position/knowledge of the viewer, the histories they bring to the text. But what children need to learn is not only an appreciation of literary qualities and form – whether in written story, media texts or more discursive modes – but also ways of relating the increasing range of their knowledge of the text's producedness to the experience and pleasure they derive from the narrative. This requires space for discussion, understanding of difference and time to develop.

The need to create space for this kind of discussion and learning is even more crucial for today's children than has been the case for previous generations. This is partly because the proliferation and effective deregulation of channels of mass com-munication via satellite, cable, computer networks, and so on mean, almost inevitably, that more children will be exposed to images and programmes designed to engender strong responses in adults at relatively earlier stages in their lives. Clearly, school should have an important role to play in enabling children to deal with their exposure to such material, through supporting the sense of choice and understanding that children are trying to develop independently. Especially crucial here is an appreci-ation of the complexity of the viewing process, particularly of the ways in which the context of viewing – who you view a programme with and in what circumstances – affects the per-ceived modality of the narrative. Communal viewing of horror movies often makes them occasions for laughter as well as thrills, for instance. They become safer, the content more emotionally distanced. All adults who have responsibilities in relation to children will wish to draw a line around what they consider safe and suitable for particular age groups. But where these lines are drawn inevitably varies widely, and a sense of the ways in which children may intuitively seek out situations for viewing programmes they are uneasy about that will make them feel safer should be helpful for adults forming judgements. Children's increasing access to highly charged and potentially disturbing visual material has become an extremely contentious issue which needs wider discussion and debate.

But a more subtle, though in some ways even more important, reason for providing children with appropriate contexts for dis-cussion and understanding of popular media forms is that these forms have themselves become increasingly complex. Adults – even teachers! – tend to be rather scornful of this complexity because they generally watch only a small proportion of the programmes that absorb children's time and attention, and where they do watch adults are likely to read off the 'types' of character and plot line dismissively as crude substitutes for their more literary adult counterparts. Yet it is undoubtedly true that popular genres for children have become increasingly sophisti-cated in the degree to which they make reference to other cul-tural forms in generating their own meanings. To draw on only one example from many possible illustrations, the hugely popu-lar (and generally despised) series *Teenage Mutant Ninja Turtles* named its heroes Raphael, Leonardo and Michelangelo. This recycling of the names of artists who have heroic status in adult cultural discourse was clearly tongue-in-cheek, but it also made available another possible level of meaning against which the narratives could be read and enjoyed. Incorporating reference to high culture in an unashamedly popular cultural form is a kind of street wit, offered up for humorous understanding. Seen in a wider context, this is also part of a commitment to a version of story-telling within which pastiche, parody, mock-homage and ironic reference to a whole range of cultural forms and icons is taken for granted. Characters may at first appear stereo-typed and one-dimensional, but the stories within which they come to life often bristle with multilevelled reference points. One has only to glance at an episode from *Sesame Street*, say, or the references made by the genie in Disney's recent version of

Aladdin to realize how pervasive this mode of presentation has become.

At one level this can be seen as an enrichment of children's culture, a mildly subversive challenge to the boundaries normally observed in the adult world. But it is dependent on the information and values recycled in this glorious postmodern *bricolage* being known, experienced and discussed in other more serious and sober contexts. Without a sense of connection to moral and social positions which are being worked out in a committed way, there is a danger that this culture may become superficial, merely wittily self-regarding. And the judgements about modality, about what to take seriously and in what degree, become increasingly complex in relation to a childhood where much unofficial learning takes place in a world of entertainment in which the themes and reference points of adult culture are recycled as forms of play, pastiche and cultural mythologizing. It is important here, clearly, not only that classrooms continue to do what they have always struggled to do well – to provide a serious context within which children can advance in a whole range of knowledges – but that there should be space for developing a critical awareness of ways in which these knowledges relate to their more playful counterparts and revisions in the visceral world of entertainment. To revert to the example of the *Ninja Turtles*, schools may well feel that they need to ensure children know who Raphael, Michelangelo and Leonardo were in their first incarnation as Renaissance artists. This is part of a common stock of knowledge, the children's cultural heritage in Western societies. What I am arguing also is that children, during the period when a majority watched the *Ninja Turtles*, would have benefited from being able to explore their perception of this popular cult series through the question of why the makers may have chosen to name their heroes in this way. Critical discriminations about levels of reality, irony and children's own position within a complex and rapidly changing culture can only be grounded if space is made available for relating knowledge and experience in such ways.

In this respect it is vital that adults should try to understand the function of popular media culture for children. Why should children be so attracted to what adults perceive as unpleasant rubbish? This question needs to be addressed seriously. I have tried to argue that this 'unpleasant rubbish' is often more sophisticated and complex than adults are willing to acknowledge. Adults often attack cult programmes for children on the grounds that they offer crude, debased representations of reality without realizing sufficiently that the modality within which these programmes operate makes them much more the stuff that dreams are made of. More specifically, they fulfil something of the function of myths in providing a pleasurable focus for major anxieties and concerns. Some 25 years ago Roland Barthes provided a seminal analysis of the way popular cultural forms in modern societies provide analogous experiences to those of myths in more traditional societies. He was drawing particularly on thinking by anthropologists such as Claude Lévi-Strauss, who had suggested that the primary function of myth in all societies was to offer stories which either reconciled or in some way resolved what was perceived in that society to be a crucial contradiction. If we bring this tradition of thinking to bear on popular media narratives for children it is possible, I think, to see them in a different light.

Power Rangers, the series which has recently provoked even more hostility than its predecessor, the *Ninja Turtles*, is an excellent example. The series draws on some fairly crude versions of traditional mythic material – forces of good and evil held together in recurrent conflict, the battle as arena within which that conflict is resolved, a plethora of monsters and enlarged, distorted hybrids of the natural world with quasi-mythological antecedents. More interesting, though, is the way the series brings into focus areas of acute contemporary anxiety and concern, masked by its heady amalgam of currently popular television forms and plot lines.

A synopsis of a single episode, drawn randomly from among hundreds of heavily formulaic and largely predictable episodes, will serve as an example:

> The six Power Rangers (who are high school pupils in ordinary life) are threatened by an evil scheme masterminded by their arch-enemy, Rita. A set of Power Ranger 'doubles' have been created who are designed to wreak havoc on community. The false Power Rangers begin with a prank – putting detergent in school drinking fountain – which results in the real Power Rangers being placed in detention for the day. More crude slapstick comedy in the detention scene even-

tually results in the Power Rangers escaping unseen, defeating their 'doubles' in combat and returning, also undetected, to complete their detention.

Emerging from the formulaic development of sequences here are a number of sites of tension and meaning that children are aware of, but for which adult culture offers no satisfactory resolution. The most obvious of these sites of contradiction is related to the issue of individual agency in a world dominated by technological systems and controls. This, indeed, is so obvious and major a feature of modern life that we have almost ceased to register it consciously other than, occasionally, as sociological cliché when some new threshold of information technology or weapons development takes place. But, as Anthony Giddens particularly has argued, it is a major feature of our modern sense of precariousness in managing identity and change on a day-to-day basis. Here, the issue is radically simplified and restored to the mythic wholeness of a life to which only celluloid superheroes can aspire by developing a format within which the power and control generated through the discipline and ancient wisdom of the martial arts is linked explicitly to technological wizardry. Within the narrative myth, the sense of anxiety generated through individuals' feeling they have no control over major issues which are increasingly managed and mediated through technological systems is dispelled by images of a bunch of school kids confidently conjuring ancient forces on computer networks. The combat scenes quite deliberately merge technological wizardry, for which a quasi-magical genesis is suggested, with the heroism of individual, hand-to-hand – or foot – conflict. The martial arts form adds the exotic aura of oriental spiritual militarism.

This combination is not exactly new. It has become a staple of science fiction writing at least since Frank Herbert's *Dune* trilogy and there have been many sorties into the form more recently in both film and television series. In a sense, the most popular of all the late-twentieth-century adventure film series, *James Bond*, could be claimed as a subcategory of this genre, and the series was in fact the subject of one of Roland Barthes' fascinating early analyses. The mythic appeal of the genre is clear. The cocktail created by merging ancient and modern forms restores a sense of the individual's control over events in a technology-dominated age. But *Power Rangers* adds to the appeal of this genre not only through the visceral realism of its use of the whole gamut of modern (an unconscious irony here?) computer-generated special effects. It also offers a fantasy form in which other major tensions can be resolved. The young adults in the series, for instance, are treated like children – they are at school, are placed in detention, are not able to argue with adults successfully for the validity of their perspective on the situation. Yet they are also more responsible, more in touch and are endowed with a greater *capacity* for dealing with any eventualities than representatives of the adult world. Their secret – the powers they can tap into and which transform them – lies in their mythic morphing capacity to resolve one of the most aching paradoxes of childhood. For modern societies promote an image of children as consumers exercising power without responsibility; while at school they are required to be responsible without power.

Clearly there are other areas within which these narratives seek to harmonize apparently powerful contradictions. The relationship between crude, slapstick, anarchically irresponsible farce and the young protagonists' more 'mature' sense of adult responsibility is significant. So too is the clash of Eastern and Western technological forces on a venture co-produced in Japan and America, which Cathy Pompe discusses in her chapter. But enough has perhaps been said to establish some of the possible functions of this popular drama as modern myth. In arguing that both the perceived weak modality of the form and the mythic functions of the narrative need to be taken account of in engaging with children's perversely enthusiastic responses, I am not suggesting that such popular series should simply be celebrated. But we do need to move beyond positions within which these narratives are seen simply as indoctrinating children or numbing their minds. Roland Barthes tried to account for the function of children's toys as offering 'essentially a microcosm of the adult world ... The fact that French toys literally prefigure the world of adult functions obviously cannot but prepare the child to accept them all.' Toys, in this view, encourage the child to accept unequivocally 'all the things the adult does not find unusual: war, bureaucracy, ugliness, Martians etc.'[1] (A touch of Gallic humour here!) But narratives such as *Power Rangers* are attractive not only because they offer normative, morally responsible roles within which the violence of the adult world can be accommodated – indeed emulated – by children. They also operate within a fantasized mode of child empowerment where children can experience their own values as purer, more coherent and more effective than the perceived 'realities' of adult power. Imaginatively they sustain an illusion of moral force within childhood which is as capable of challenging adult complacency as of engendering conformity. They are not merely 'mind-numbing' or automatically conservative, and the kind of critical reflection which classrooms seek to promote needs to take account of this.

Any worthwhile educational practice that seeks to engage productively with the narratives that absorb so much of children's attention must open up space for critical reflection as a central goal. But the terms within which critical reflection takes place are likely to vary wildly between adult and child audiences. Children tolerate – indeed require – experiences they find important or pleasurable being repeated to an extent that few adults can bear. What appears formulaic, reductive or absurd to adults may operate as a kind of time fault, locking generations out of each other's experiences. Children, by this means, are provided with an imaginative theatre within which they can test the possibility of conflicting issues they are learning to cope with being magically harmonized. In this respect the myths which popular children's narratives ritually re-enact may operate as horizons of hope, promoting the illusion of an adult world that must come to terms with the moral force of child fantasy, rather than the other way around. That these horizons of hope are so often spliced with the kind of techno-aggression which adults experience as a threat to childhood innocence is a problem, though whether for children or adults is perhaps debatable. Certainly, this perspective has absorbed adult critical attention to the virtual exclusion of potentially more positive – or complex – perceptions. In the end, it is what children make of these stories which is most important, where they lead. In supporting children's developing critical consciousness I do not, of course, mean to imply that children should learn to disparage what has been of importance for them. Clearly, they will eventually outgrow their need for this particular format and may themselves come to parody, or take much further the conventions represented here. In seeking to understand more about the ways in which children make use of such popular genres, teachers should not be seeking to colonize such material for the classroom. Rather, the aim is to create opportunities for children to make use of the kinds of knowledge they are developing independently within a curriculum which, though it may continue to prioritize the written word, is no longer aligned with 'a view of English that fundamentally neglects the experiences and competencies of the vast majority of young people'.[2]

NOTES

1 Roland Barthes, *Mythologies*, London: Paladin, 1973, p. 53.
2 David Buckingham and Julian Sefton-Green, *Cultural Studies Goes to School*, London: Taylor & Francis, 1994, p. 217.

FURTHER READING

On the theoretical background to modality and linguistics:
Bob Hodge and David Tripp, *Children and Television* (1986, Polity Press, Cambridge). A fuller discussion of the linguistic background in Gunter Kress and Bob Hodge, *Ideology and Language* is also very interesting and has been influential.

On understanding what children themselves say about television:
There is a particularly wide-ranging discussion, based on extensive research and including some illuminating transcripts of interviews with children in David Buckingham, *Children Talking Television* (1993, The Falmer Press, London). Charles Sarland, *Young People Reading: Culture and Response* (1991, Open University Press, Buckingham) deals mainly with rather older children, but has useful chapters on horror genres especially. Finally, Kathleen McDonnell, *Kid Culture – Children and Adults and Popular Culture* offers an insightful review of much of the material currently engaging children, combined with a lively, positive assessment of its value. The work is based on North American culture, but most of the examples apply equally in Britain.

On applications to work in classrooms:
There have been a number of excellent books and articles over the past ten years particularly. Most recently, David Buckingham and Julian Sefton-Green, *Cultural Studies Goes to School* (1994, Taylor & Francis, London), though it deals with rather older children, has been especially useful in trying to reassess the value of what children can learn in this area. Carol Craggs, *Media Education in the Primary School* (1992, Routledge, London) brings a wide-ranging theoretical background to bear on practical suggestions for classroom work and Chapter 5, 'Representations of Reality', picks up on a number of the themes I have explored here.

Part II

Ways of working

In the next two chapters we focus closely on children and teachers in primary schools working with the themes, ideas and products of the popular culture industry and we examine in detail how children's literate ideas and textual knowledge can be developed in school with a model of literacy that works with growing consciousness. In Chapter 3 Helen Bromley explores and demonstrates how much understanding relevant to school-based literacy practices young children gain from watching the narrative videos that have been intended and designed for children. Through empirical work with very young children, she shows how they can, given the opportunity, apply rich knowledge gained from watching videos to such school language and literacy practices as detailed in the National Curriculum: speaking and listening, reading and writing. The thrust of her argument is that in learning and developing all these practices, reception children are already active and critical viewers, not just passive watchers of videos, and are already deft manipulators of a sophisticated visual literacy. She develops her argument through evidence gleaned from further discussions and work with 6- and 7-year-old children who have seen a variety of videos. She goes on to show how teachers can build on the knowledge and experience of film that children bring with them into school, by creating for children an environment where the products of popular culture can be used as a shared context for developing and making sense of many traditional school-based literacy practices.

In Chapter 4 Cathy Pompe focuses closely on the role and potentialities of popular culture products and narratives with children in the middle years of primary school. Based on detailed empirical work with a group of 8- and 9-year-olds, she shows how children play and position themselves within their worlds, using layers of meaning and knowledge gleaned from television, comics, videos and toys. Through looking closely and sympathetically at the children's constructions of meanings, which variously incorporate, use, reject and creatively transform different aspects of their cultural experiences outside school, she points to how they may be helped to articulate and embellish this knowledge inside the curriculum. Again, she indicates that a model of literacy which respects and enriches their growing experience of the world is a more empowering and relevant approach than one which fails to listen to and help them develop their own voices.

Chapter 3

'Did you know that there's no such thing as Never Land?'

Working with video narratives in the early years

Helen Bromley

Emily approached me as I was showing a prospective parent around the school. She took me by the hand and led me to a quiet part of the classroom. 'Come here, Mrs Bromley', she said, 'I've got something to tell you.' I bent down to listen and Emily carefully explained that she had just discovered that Never Land, home of Peter Pan, was not actually a real place. I asked her how she felt about this. 'Very sad', she replied, 'I was hoping to save up and go there one day.' This short conversation is just one example of how the culture of video watching pervades the lives of and influences the children in the school where I teach. Video watching is mentioned by the children on a daily basis, usually to link something that they have seen on video to the learning that is taking place in school. The link is usually preceded by the phrase, 'I've got that on my video'. This natural behaviour clearly demonstrates that young children can learn much from the videos that they watch and that they can make such knowledge explicit. Those who work with young children should take account of such wisdom and make space in their classrooms for it to be explored and extended.

The majority of videos that are mentioned by the children are those produced by the Walt Disney Corporation or the BBC. Most of the children in my class have a large collection of videos, including feature-length cartoons that have been released in such a format. It is these animated feature films that provide the context for shared discussion amongst the children, because ownership is common to many of them. Parents clearly support the watching of these videos and have mentioned to me how much they enjoy watching them themselves. In this chapter I intend to demonstrate that teachers can create an atmosphere in which knowledge gained from watching videos can be used to lessen tensions between home-based and school-based literary practices.

My thinking in this area has been particularly influenced by the work of Tizard and Hughes (1984) and Shirely Brice Heath (1983). Both of these studies have shown that there can be enormous differences between literacy practices at home and at school. Shirley Brice Heath argues that, 'Long before school, their language and *culture* at home has structured for them the meanings which will give shape to their experiences in classrooms and beyond' (1983: 368; my italics).

For my daughter, and the vast majority of the children that I teach, videos form part of this culture and are integral to ways in which meanings are made. This was brought home to me when, one evening, we had a family outing to a fish and chip restaurant. Looking up at the menu where it said 'Plaice and Haddock Combo, £4.25', Becky said 'What's a combo?' Before I could form an adequate reply, she said, 'Oh, I know – in *Aladdin*, the Genie says, "What about that fez and vest combo; much too 3rd century." It must be two things together!'

The video culture was also much in evidence when I was privileged to be able to make visits to the homes of the reception class children. Whatever differences existed between the homes, they all had one thing in common, and that was video ownership. Videos were strewn about the floor, or sat alongside books on the shelves or in their own cabinet. In one home, Callum was watching *Thomas the Tank Engine* on video, whilst he played the story out in front of the TV with his road mat and toy engines. The story involved a trip to the woods and as Callum played, he related the story of a trip that he had made to the woods with his mum, matching his experiences to Thomas's.

Observing my own daughter's literacy development provided rich evidence to support the argument that home literacy practices are crucial to a child's intellectual development. She has been an avid video watcher since she was a toddler, and it became apparent to me that, far from being a passive watcher, she was becoming an extremely critical viewer. There was also another aspect to this video watching. Not only was she becoming a critical viewer, she was also absorbing lessons about language which may have been traditionally regarded as the preserve of school-based learning. These included sight vocabulary, the acquisition of known texts and the skills of prediction and comprehension. I noticed that she watched many of her videos in order to commit them to memory and then took great delight in joining in the next time that they were played. (*The Sound of Music* is one example of this, where she managed to portray all seven Von Trapp children by herself – no mean achievement!) Having had my consciousness raised in this way, I then began to look very carefully at the children I taught, and I realized that knowledge gained from watching videos was being incorporated into my classroom on a daily basis.

At the same time as all this was taking place, I was becoming aware of the need to redefine what I had traditionally regarded as 'reading'. Although the children in my class were being offered a broad range of reading material in the form of high-quality pictorial texts, I began to realize that there was far more to reading than that contained within the covers of a book. Outside the classroom there was a whole world of reading at which children were succeeding, without instruction from the teacher. A study of environmental print that I carried out with 4½-year-old children, clearly demonstrated that they had no problem differentiating between McDonald's and Burger King, or the Early Learning Centre and Toys 'Я' Us. This type of reading took place in a meaningful and purposeful context, just like my daughter choosing between *Peter Pan* and *Beauty and the Beast* from the rows of videos in the video cabinet. It was apparent that young children were reading a whole variety of texts outside school and I became determined to discover ways of recognizing these literacies in my classroom.

This chapter is the story of how the realizations outlined above came to be put into practice in the classroom. I intend to show how infant-aged children have made use of the video culture in school, most particularly in the areas of speaking and listening, reading and writing.

SPEAKING AND LISTENING

For all that my growing years were full of books and texts, there were also other voices.

(Meek, 1991: 235)

In *On Being Literate* Meek (1991) argues that the nature of literacy is constantly shifting, and that what it means to be literate is dependent on the social, economic and historical context into which we are born. Each individual will have their own particular literary history, a collection of memories unique to them, that will inform their learning. Each literacy event in which we participate represents a dialogue with others; with the authors of the texts for which we have been the audience. Texts must be taken to have a definition wider than books or journals. For today's children there are a myriad of technologies to be read, computers and videos being just two of them. Children need to know that what counts as reading and writing at home will also be valued at school, and vice versa, so that there is not a constantly changing shift in context and purpose for their literary activities. Videos provide a wide range of 'other voices'; if the children are prepared and ready to listen to them, then so should we be.

One of the main differences between watching a video at home rather than at school is that at home you are allowed to talk. In fact, talking whilst watching a video is an integral part of the enjoyment and understanding of it. Such talk provides opportunities to reflect on the story line, discuss favourite scenes, reminisce about situations in which the film has first been seen, and much more. In my experience, this is not often the case in school. Teachers usually expect children to watch in silence, and the content and focus of the ensuing discussion is teacher-controlled. It is possible to change this situation so that, through discussion and debate, children's thinking about a variety of concepts can be moved on and their knowledge about a broad range of issues made explicit.

A group of my reception infants had watched two videos telling the story of Robin Hood. One was that produced by Walt Disney, the other was part of a series called 'Animated Classics'. The quality of discussion was extremely high. The children clearly demonstrated interpretations of the plot, knowledge of motive and characterization and skills of prediction. During the watching of the Disney film, children commented on the range of instruments used in the soundtrack – 'I think I can hear a violin, Mrs Bromley' – and the purpose of their use – 'Violins always make you feel creepy'. What I found particularly remarkable about such comments was that they came from children about whom it would have been easy to make wrongful assumptions. They were not the children I would most expect to have knowledge of orchestral instruments and their uses. I was wrong to assume that there are limited contexts in which such knowledge could be gained.

The sharing of knowledge was particularly apparent between children who had seen the video before and those who had not. The predictions were based on the animation, not on the words spoken. Facial expression was particularly important in informing the predictions, as this seemed to give the information required to build up knowledge of a particular character's personality and therefore the actions that he or she was likely to take. Danny, who had obviously seen the film frequently, advised his neighbour as to the characters of King John and his side-kick, the snake (Sir Hiss), and this child then began to make predictions about the plot, not having seen the film before.

Many questions were directed at me. For example, 'Do you like the snake, Mrs Bromley?', 'Which is your favourite bit?', and a lot of questioning that centred around the children trying to understand why Robin had avoided drowning by having a piece of hollow reed in his mouth. What struck me as exceptionally important about this dialogue was the fact that the questions were child-initiated – it was not simply a case of me asking questions to which I already knew the answer. This is particularly significant because, as I have already said, there are differences between home and school literacy practices. One difference is that children's asking of questions is a naturally occurring activity at home, but at school the questions demanded of the teacher are likely to be far fewer (Tizard and Hughes, 1984; Wells, 1986; Edwards and Mercer, 1987).

It was during the watching of the second (poorer quality) video that I became even more convinced, not only of the value of talk surrounding video watching but of its potential to unlock areas of knowledge of which the teacher may otherwise be unaware. The children were able to compare and contrast the standards of the two videos in a very sophisticated manner. They discussed the quality of the pictures, the soundtrack and the plot. Their absorption in the discussion was total; no-one interrupted with an inappropriate comment, instead they behaved like a panel of experts. They were able to comment critically on such features as the range of instruments used in the soundtrack and the way in which it failed to match the movements of the characters. This, they felt, contrasted sharply with the Disney video, where the soundtrack is one of the highlights of the film. Cheryl felt that the music was too slow: 'There aren't any songs that you can join in with.' For Dean, the problem lay with the synchronization of talk and animation: 'The movement of their lips doesn't match what they're saying.' The quality of the soundtrack was further criticized by Kieron: 'You can't hear what they're saying.'

This critical ability has not been taught to them by anyone in school. It was a natural behaviour for them. They were in fact sharing knowledge about the videos they were watching. This sharing of information is an example of the social construction of knowledge and understanding outlined by Vygotsky: 'Human learning presupposes a specific social nature and process by which children grow into the intellectual life of those around them' (Vygotsky, 1978: 26). This was certainly true of the discourse outlined above. The children had all previously watched videos at their own home (or someone else's), and in these circumstances discussion of its features would have been part of the context of viewing. As mentioned earlier, this is usually one of the differences between viewing at home and school. As many of the group had seen the film before, a collective memory was in existence. For this reason, the children had no problem positioning themselves in the discourse, as it was a discourse type with which they were very familiar. This meant that they were able, even at such a young age, to take control of the discussion – the turn-taking, evaluating and questioning were in their own hands. It should be emphasized that this did not arise as the result of an agenda that had been set by the teacher, but rather because the children were allowed to address their own concerns.

Role-play is another area of the talk curriculum where I have seen videos make a significant contribution. My daughter arrived home from school one evening full of anticipation for the next day. It transpired that this was not because of any school-directed activity but rather because, 'We're playing this really good game in the playground.' The game was entitled 'The Land Before Time' and was based on the video of the same name. The promotional material describes this as 'a tale of hope, survival and love' which will teach 'unforgettable lessons about life and sticking together'. Discussing the game with her showed that lessons *had* been learned, perhaps even more valuable than those suggested by its makers. Importantly, it was necessary to have seen the video before you were allowed to play the game. The common knowledge that was provided by the collective experience of seeing the video gave the children a shared mental context from which to start their game. Edwards and Mercer describe context as a 'property of the general understandings that obtain between people who communicate' (1987: 63). The children had all seen the video, so many things could be taken as understood. To include someone who had not seen the film would have involved them in time-wasting explanations – time when they could have been getting on with their game. The children had created an imaginary world in the playground, using locations from the video. They were not, however, re-enacting the film but rewriting it with many original ideas. A great deal of planning was required for the next day's play and it was apparent that the children found it very easy to slip in and out of the game. I asked my daughter if she felt that there was any way in which playing the game could help her with her work in class. Her reply was, 'I think that it helps you with the past, the present and the future of thought.' Playing the video-inspired game was helping her to reflect on prior knowledge, speculate on possible outcomes and use both of these actions to support the task in hand. This serves as a powerful reminder of the importance of narrative.

This role-play not only takes place in the playground but also, if valued by the teacher, in the classroom. I was invited by a colleague to watch a play of *Aladdin* that some of her class had put together. This was part of a series of productions that was to include *Peter Pan* and *Cinderella*. As with the older children, membership of the group was dependent on having seen the film. In fact, one child was heard to state, 'I own the video, so I'm in charge' (as the play progressed, it became apparent that this would come under negotiation, and although Rebecca thought she was 'in charge' because of ownership, the children themselves looked to Jamie as their leader and decision-maker). It is wrong to assume that a large number of children were excluded from a part in the play. The rest of the class were quite used to this particular group's theatrical productions and enjoyed being the audience. They were in a class where all children were held in high regard whatever their particular talents, and this overrode the need for all children to be in every play.

The influence of the video on the content of the play was indisputable. The characters took their names from those in the film: Princess Jasmine, Iago (the parrot), the evil Jafahl and Abu the monkey do not owe their origin to *1001 Nights*. Whole snatches of speech were taken from the screenplay, interspersed with their own additions. One child had a role that was crucial to the success of the play – Jamie was the production manager, he was also the stage manager, costume designer and make-up artist all rolled into one. He obviously had the greatest knowledge of the script and would support the others if they were uncertain of what to do next. The whole play was an excellent example of how play can provide opportunities for collaborative learning as described by Bruner:

> I have come increasingly to recognize that most learning in most settings is a communal activity, a sharing of the culture. It isn't just that the child must make his knowledge his own, but that he must make it his own in a community of those who share his sense of culture. It is this that leads me to emphasize not only discovery and invention but also the importance of offering and sharing.
>
> (Bruner, 1986: 127)

All of this was apparent in the children's play. The culture being shared was that of the video – all the children accepted it as a valuable stimulus for play, providing the basis for negotiation and sharing. Discovery and invention took place in many forms: the construction of props (magic lamps constructed entirely from paper and tape), the improvisation of the costumes and the innovative ways in which the plot was embellished. The most amusing example of this was Jamie, in the role of Abu, taking a shower and singing at the same time. It was very funny, and owed nothing to Walt Disney's plot. Each time he rehearsed this particular scene there were great cries from the other children of 'more' and 'let's have that again, Jamie!' It was an opportunity for the children to display their tacit knowledge of the powerful uses to which language can be put, in an extremely enjoyable context. It was crucial that the teacher held this role-play in high regard and created an atmosphere in which it could take place and be valued by the whole classroom community.

READING

> The test of modern literacy is to be able to read *new* texts.
>
> (Meek, 1991: 36; my italics)

I am arguing here for reading to be seen as an essentially social activity, where collaboration and risk-taking are encouraged. For the vast majority of adult learners, opportunities to look closely at a text and discuss its possible meanings as part of a group are deliberately provided. For children, such opportunities may occur naturally at home, as part of the bedtime story ritual, for example, but may not always be replicated in schools. Children should, I feel, be given ample scope to discuss texts that they have read with each other. This is crucially important because, as Vygotsky (1986) argues, talk is essential to concept formation. This talk takes place in a social context, before the concepts are internalized by the individual. Thus, children who are able to discuss their reading with each other will master ideas that will form the basis for their future thinking and construction of meaning. This is true whether the children are 'reading' a book, a comic or a video. Visual literacy is crucially important to the children of today, whether on the printed page or on celluloid.

Gathered together were a group of children who had seen a video version of *Not Now Bernard* by David McKee. They had also read the book. They began to compare the experience of watching a video to that of reading a book. The ensuing discussion was very enlightening. They enjoyed the video for the sound effects, the moving pictures and the different voices. Their criticisms of the video were of a highly sophisticated nature. When asked if there were any disadvantages to the video version (as compared to reading the book), one child replied, 'You can't pore over a video like you can a book. Well, you can, you can press pause, but all those funny lines come up and spoil it.'

Re-reading portions of text was also deemed preferable to re-watching, which, it was felt, was hindered by the technology involved (rewinding, difficulty in isolating the portion to be re-watched, etc.). Most of the children felt that books were better at helping you learn to read, although some of them thought that books and videos used together were a good idea as 'you could learn the book from the video and then read it yourself'. These children obviously had no problem with the notion of 'scaffolded learning' (Bruner, 1986) or the theory of the 'zone of proximal development' (Vygotsky, 1986). Vygotsky argued that through working in the company of those more experienced than themselves it is possible for children to acquire new skills. Scaffolding a task involves engaging in a dialogue through which the learner is able to extend their own thinking. Hence, collaboration and talk become crucial. Talk is the tool through which new understandings are constructed, new meanings made and learning is handed over. There was strong evidence of this in the discussion that followed.

One child felt that she preferred books if there was something that you found interesting or did not understand, because you were able to take the book with you to discuss the point with someone. Here was a child who had grasped the notion of the shared context for discussion. One little boy described how he loved his videos to relax with, but that he got more involved with a book because, 'Well, you have to read the words, don't you Mrs Bromley.' The children also described how it was possible to do other things whilst watching a video, which was not possible if you were reading a book.

They did not want to be without either medium, feeling that one complemented and supported the other. Asked what they thought were the advantages of a video over a book, one girl described it as a 'new way of seeing'. This was a phenomenal comment for a child of 6 to make. It is apparent from this that children are able to theorize about their own literacy practices.

The children were making explicit ways in which videos, far from discouraging or replacing reading, actually increased their access to written texts. Shirley Brice Heath states that,

> children have to learn to select, hold and retrieve content from books and other written or printed texts in accordance with their community's rules or ways of taking, and the children's learning follows community paths of socialisation.
>
> (Heath, 1983: 49)

'Ways of taking' are the ways in which children derive meaning from the environment around them. Some of these ways will match those traditionally used in school; others will not. For these children there will be a mismatch and a chance that they will not be able to make their prior knowledge visible in school.

For these children, videos form one of the ways of taking. That is, videos are one of the forms of literacy in the community that surrounds our school, acceptable as a shared activity for adults and children alike. Through watching videos and discussing them with the members of their community, children learn much about the structure of narrative and visual representation. It is for this reason that it is important for teachers to recognize the significance of the child's pre-school experience of videos and not regard it as less valuable than traditional school-based literacy practices.

Frank Smith (1988) describes how children benefit from joining a 'literacy club'. Membership of this 'club' is automatic. Children join the club of language users that they expect they will be like. Experienced members of the club expect to have to support those less experienced than themselves (this links with the notions of the zone of proximal development and scaffolded learning outlined earlier). It is important to note that children are not just learning the mechanics of reading – sight vocabulary, decoding skills, etc. – they are also learning what reading *means* in their particular community. They absorb a culture, and video watching is part of this culture.

Children who have had experience of watching videos are members of a visual literacy club, which fulfils all the characteristics of learning through club membership outlined by Smith (1988: 6–9). Redefined in terms of a video, these are:

- The experience is meaningful; the content of the video is always presented in a meaningful manner, whether fact or fiction. It is never nonsensical or disjointed.
- Watching a video always has a point; whether to relive a memorable experience or explore a new one.
- Watching a video is effortless, not a testing situation with its associated stress.
- Learning that takes place during the watching of a video is incidental rather than intentional. I realize that parents may purchase videos deliberately as a method of educating the child on some particular point, but I am referring here to the learning that takes place during the watching of narrative videos.

- Videos are most often watched in a social context, either with family or friends. Some members of that group are likely to be more experienced watchers than others. This provides the social and collaborative base for learning outlined by Vygotsky.

- Videos provide the ideal opportunity for the vicarious learning which Smith argues is one of the great benefits of club membership. They contain a vast range of models of types of language construction: dialects, accents, tones of voice, sentence construction, jokes, to name but a few. These provide models for the children to copy or mimic in their everyday lives.

- The seventh aspect of club membership, as outlined by Smith, is that it should be free from the risks of punishment, failure or embarrassment. I would say that watching the sort of videos encompassed by this chapter would not entail the children taking such risks. This is not to negate the value of all risk-taking. Rather like reading a book with which they become emotionally engaged, children will wonder about outcomes, even on repeated viewings, but in the knowledge that they are themselves safe from danger.

This notion of club membership was used explicitly by the children in the role-play outlined earlier.

Videos provide an opportunity for reading a variety of texts and symbols. Young children are able to identify the voice behind, and the audience for, the text on the box in which the video is contained. The cover of any video contains a mass of information in the form of words, pictures, numerals and symbols. The children who I worked with were able to identify the author, audience and motives of the text.

The children were asked to identify something from the cover that they had to read, whether it was words or a picture or a symbol. After they had done this, I then asked them questions regarding purpose, audience and motive. They analysed the text thus:

'Beauty and the Beast' [the title]   This was instantly identified as the title of the film, put on the box by the Walt Disney Company so that everyone would know which film it was. 'Everyone' included parents, children, video store owners, both retail and rental, as well as the owners of stores like

Woolworth's. The children also noticed that the style in which the title was printed carried messages about the characters in the film. 'Beauty' is written in a flowing style, delicate in nature, while the word 'Beast' is portrayed in manly capital letters.

'Disney's enchanting Oscar winning classic'   The children knew that this portion of the text was to tell you that the film had won an award. They felt that the purpose of putting this on the box was so that more people would buy it. Very astute! They also noticed the tiny letter © by the word Oscar, and were able not only to find it on other parts of the video box, but also to refer to other contexts in which they had seen it used.

The picture of Mrs Potts   This was seen along with the other pictures on the box, as giving lots of information about the content of the film, especially for people who have not seen it before. The children felt that the pictures gave clues as to the characters in the film and to the nature of their personalities. One little boy felt that it was important that the baddies were illustrated, because that shows that 'there will be exciting bits in it'. Significantly, the pictures were seen as being particularly useful for those 'who couldn't read yet'. This was felt to be particularly true of the pictures on the spine, which enabled the viewer/purchaser to select the video that they required even if they were unable to read the words.

The bar code   The children were all well aware of the purpose of the bar code, i.e., that it held information regarding price. It was their identification of the readership that was most interesting. They knew, not only that the intended readership of a bar code was a machine, but also that it could be a variety of machines: 'A pen thing, a thing with a handle, and a beam of light at the checkout.'

What this investigation shows is that, far from replacing reading, videos provide opportunities for reading texts from a variety of genre. The reading is contextualized, meaningful and purposeful. The video cover is teaching some very valuable lessons about reading.

Margaret Meek writes:

If literacy includes, as I believe it must, *reflection* on what is written to be read, then irrespective of changes in the technologies of the new literacies, the composers and receivers of communications and texts of words and images, will have to be more *critically* literate . . . Our children will still have to read texts in contexts and in ways they will need to understand.

(Meek, 1991: 208; my italics)

The evidence quoted above clearly demonstrates that children have the ability to be *critical* readers of the materials presented to them and are not merely a passive audience of (in this case) the Disney publicity machine.

The type of reading taking place when children look at the cover on the video box is not the same as that required to read narrative. There is no right or wrong order in which to read the information, although the parts do form a coherent whole. It is still possible for the children to scrutinize small pieces of this (the bar code, for example) and read them in isolation. These are reading skills which will be required to read a variety of texts, including non-fiction texts, which require the ability to skim and scan for specific pieces of information across pages heavily laden with different images. Videos appear to be providing children with a bridge from which to cross into other texts.

WRITING

Our new situation is characterised by mixed, hybrid, modes of talking and writing that include pictures and looking.

(Meek, 1991: 231)

There is no doubt that my daughter is faced with acquiring a different set of literacies to those that I was brought up with, both in school and at home. When I was at primary school in the 1960s, computers were still regarded as the stuff of science fiction or the property of large corporations. I never dreamt that one day I would use, let alone own one. To my daughter, computer literacy is part of everyday life, as are CD-ROMs. During the writing of this chapter, I have seen advertisements on TV for 'computer televisions', yet another innovation. The notion of what constitutes 'writing' is regarded as fluid by the publishers of this book, as my contract contains a clause which uses the phrase 'all forms of media, whether now in existence or yet to be invented'.

Writing is part of a child's literary environment in many

different forms and, depending on the community from which they come, children will have experienced a wide range of writing practices before they come to school. If teachers ignore this and subscribe to a 'monolithic model of what writing is and what it leads to' (Scriber and Cole, quoted in Czerniewska, 1992: 10) then it will be difficult to understand how watching videos supports the development of writing. It is necessary to widen the definition of written literacy. Czerniewska herself argues that 'new ways of constructing literacy are particularly evident at times when technological innovations introduce new patterns of interaction with print' (1992: 10). Videos are one such innovation. They provide many opportunities for interactions with print, which may not be immediately obvious.

As outlined above, the video cover provides examples of a wide variety of written texts. Children see letters in many fonts, the print on the video providing a model for their own emergent efforts. Temple *et al.* say that:

> Discovering how to write English involves making choices from a large range of alternatives. Children may very well be more aware of the alternatives than adults are, because our long experience with alphabetic writing tends to blind us to the possibility that there may be more ways of representing words with symbols that are different from the ways we do it.
>
> (quoted in Czerniewska, 1992: 32)

Children are not able to make choices if a variety of possibilities have not been made available to them. Videos do just that.

The print contained, not only on the cover of the video, but also in the context of the film itself helps to teach that print conveys meaning. This is done in ways that are designed to attract the viewer's interest. (Anyone who doubts that this is the case should view the sequence in Walt Disney's *Aladdin* where the genie introduces himself.) Print becomes associated with pleasurable activities. The print on videos is contextualized and no doubt forms one of the occasions 'in which a piece of writing is integral to the nature of the participants' reactions and their interpretive processes' (Heath quoted in Czerniewska, 1992).

I would reiterate my belief that video watching is essentially a social activity. The child may not permanently be in the company of others but, if my home is anything to go by, anybody who happens to be about at the time can get involved in discussion about the video, whether or not they have seen it all.

If children are aware of the authorship of videos then they can learn valuable lessons about the products of authorship. One of the main consequences of video watching is the widening of the definition of what counts as a literacy event.

I have a small amount of evidence to suggest that the content of children's stories may be influenced by watching videos. Carol Fox (1993) quotes a study by Sutton-Smith which found that, in school, children drew extensively on TV material for their stories. This was because the programmes were culturally shared by the children. In the instance outlined below, videos were the common culture.

After hearing the story 'The Frog Prince Continued' the children were invited to write their own continued story, from a fairy tale of their own choice. Many of the children chose to continue the story of 'Beauty and the Beast'. This was the Disney cartoon most recently released for home ownership and many of them had received it as a Christmas present. I am convinced that the popularity of the video and its availability for ownership influenced the children's choice of story, as it is not a fairy story that is well known by young children. Classic fairy-tales such as 'Goldilocks and the Three Bears' and 'Red Riding Hood' were ignored in favour of those on video, including 'The Little Mermaid' and 'Cinderella'. It is important for teachers to realize that the fact that many children chose the same title for their story provided the opportunity for collaborative learning to take place. I have known times in my career when I would have been displeased because so many of the children had chosen to do the same story. This attitude was inappropriate here. In choosing similar themes, the children had created for themselves a shared context for discussion. The children were explicitly told that they could talk about their work with each other. Bereiter and Scardamalia argue that:

> solo composing practices required for writing are far different from the conversations that children will have experienced. Conversations are usually centred around familiar topics and are supported by what others are saying and by cues in the context.

> (Quoted in Czerniewska, 1992: 95)

In this instance, the video was the familiar context and the conversations that they had about their work meant that emphasis was not on the solitary composition of a piece of work but rather on a shared experience. As Frank Smith says, 'The ability to write alone comes with experience and is not always easy or necessary' (quoted in CLPE 1990: 18).

IMPLICATIONS FOR TEACHERS

The implications of this work lie far beyond the supplying of a few ideas for using videos in the classroom. There are principles underlying this work which are central to the development of children as thinkers and learners. Margaret Meek states that 'comparative studies show that literacy is locally learned, yet claims are made for teaching methods as universals' (Meek, 1993: 92).

Through looking closely at what children learn from watching videos, I have come to recognize the importance of the literary experiences that children bring with them to school. Acknowledgement of the existence of such experiences is not enough. I feel that teachers must find ways to make explicit to children that such knowledge is valued and can be used in the school context. It is not only for the benefit of the children; I found that the time I spent working in this way was one of the most exciting periods in my career. I feel that I benefited because I found out so much about what the children I was teaching already knew.

In watching videos at home children have been taking part in a certain kind of literacy event. These events set the pattern for the child's subsequent interpretation of the printed word. Shirley Brice Heath states that:

> Patterns of language use in any community are in accord with and reinforce other cultural patterns, such as space and time orderings, problem solving techniques, group loyalties and preferred patterns of recreation.

> (Heath 1983: 344)

All this is evident in my observations; Becky's description of the past, present and future of thought, designing props for *Aladdin*, membership of the play being decided by which videos had been seen and Adam's statement that he liked his videos to relax with.

> One important function of education may be described as cognitive socialisation... within a society the education system has its own epistemological culture. This culture and the institutional framework within which the children are educated, are what distinguishes education from other types of learning.
>
> (Edwards and Mercer, 1987: 161)

If teachers are to make cognitive socialization of children effective then they must create through joint action and discussion a contextual framework for educational activities. The shared mental context of the narrative structure of a particular video is one way in which this can be achieved; the teacher watching with the children and sharing their concerns, or through children creating opportunities for learning such as *Aladdin*. I believe that the benefits of such activities are aptly described by Griffin and Cole, when they state that:

> Social organization and leading activities provide a gap within which the child can develop a novel creative analysis... a zone of proximal development is a dialogue between the child and his future; it is not a dialogue between the child and an adult's past.
>
> (Griffin and Cole quoted in Edwards and Mercer, 1987: 164)

This was particularly apparent during the production of *Aladdin* described earlier. Jamie acted as facilitator for the whole group. He organized and led them extremely effectively. Anyone who has listened to children's play will recall the type of dialogue outlined by Griffin and Cole. It consists of the 'What if we...?' 'Supposing you...' This is the dialogue between the child and his future.

As Bruner says:

> The language of education, if it is to be an invitation to reflection and culture creating, cannot be the so called language of objectivity. It must express stance and counter stance and in the process leave place for reflection, for meta cognition. It is this that permits one to reach the higher ground,

this process of objectifying in language or image what one has thought and then turning around and reconsidering it.

(Bruner, 1986: 129)

All children, whatever their circumstances, should have the opportunity to reach the 'higher ground'. They should be able to reach it by familiar paths, not those which have been artificially created by the education system. Videos provide one such pathway. The nature of videos invites reflection and reconsideration. They are watched repeatedly because there is something new to be found in each watching. They encourage children to share, negotiate and compare their views with each other because of the shared context. Valuing the kinds of literacy events that the child has experienced at home gives the teacher a range of wonderful opportunities for seeing knowledge made explicit. This must surely lead to more effective teaching and learning.

A unilateral view of what is to count as worthwhile knowledge and of how it is to be constructed undervalues the contributions that children can make in terms of their own experience, interests and method of inquiry, thereby impoverishing the learning experience.

(Wells, 1986: 219)

I believe it is crucial that teachers take into account children's interests and concerns when planning activities that are to take place in school. Videos constitute a large part of the child's preschool experience and undoubtedly contribute to the meanings that they make. I am not suggesting that teachers take the video culture and attempt to dominate it with predetermined concerns, far from it. Instead, we should leave children in no doubt that we value their knowledge and expertise, and we should offer opportunities to use them.

CONCLUSION

Hannah is sitting on the classroom floor, leafing through the Dorling Kindersley book of *Amazing Snakes*. She pauses at the page showing the cobra: 'Mrs Bromley, I've found Jafahl's snake', she says. She is correct.

I am reading the book called *The Whales Song*, by Diane Sheldon, to the reception class when Jodie points out the similarity between the imagery on its cover and pictures from Walt Disney's *The Lion King*.

A parent has brought two kittens into school for us to look at. Someone wants to know if the kittens can swim. One boy replies, 'Cats can't swim, I know. I've got *Homeward Bound*, the cat couldn't swim in *Homeward Bound*.'

Remarks like those quoted above happen on a daily basis, evidence of children relating knowledge gained from watching videos to everyday school life. Videos provide a wealth of experiences from which children can construct new meanings. The video culture has pervaded all aspects of language.

If you still regard viewing as a passive activity, reflect on the last few experiences that you have had with videos. You will have laughed, cried, been frightened or provoked and almost certainly you will have had a discussion with someone about it. Through discussion you may have come to a greater understanding of what you have seen or enjoyed laughing at a shared joke.

Looking closely at such experiences, those of my daughter and of the children I teach, has been tremendously exciting. It has confirmed for me the belief that children bring with them a wealth of knowledge to school. This knowledge is gained from interaction with a wide variety of texts, ever increasing in complexity and sophistication. I am not suggesting that teachers appropriate the children's out-of-school pleasures for school use, rather, that we look closely at how we can provide opportunities for children to demonstrate their knowledge to us. However, demonstration alone is not enough. It is critically important that children are allowed to use what they have already learned in the joint creation of new meanings.

I asked my daughter if she thought that videos would ever be superseded. What would be better than videos? Her reply: 'Well, the only thing that would be better, would be if the characters could come out of the film and talk to you.' Perhaps, one day, they will.

FURTHER READING

Bearne, E. (ed.) (1995) *Greater Expectations: Children Reading Writing,* London: Cassell.

Buckingham, D. (1993) *Children Talking Television: The Making of Television Literacy,* London: Falmer Press.

Styles, M., Bearne, E. and Watson, V. (1992) *After Alice,* London: Cassell.

Styles, M., Bearne, E. and Watson, V. (1994) *The Prose and the Passion,* London: Cassell.

BIBLIOGRAPHY

Bruner, J. (1986) *Actual Minds, Possible Worlds,* Cambridge, Mass: Harvard University Press.

CLPE (1990) *Shared Reading, Shared Writing,* London: Centre for Language in Primary Education.

Czerniewska, P. (1992) *Learning About Writing,* Oxford: Blackwell.

Edwards, D. and Mercer, N. (1987) *Common Knowledge: The Development of Understanding in the Classroom,* London: Routledge.

Fox, C. (1993) *At the Very Edge of the Forest,* London: Cassell.

Heath, S. B. (1983) *Ways With Words: Language, Life and Work in Communities and Classrooms,* Cambridge: Cambridge University Press.

Meek, M. (1991) *On Being Literate,* London: The Bodley Head.

Meek, M. (1993) *The Politics of Reading,* Cambridge: University of Cambridge and Homerton College, Cambridge.

Smith, F. (1988) *Joining the Literacy Club,* Portsmouth: Heinemann.

Tizard, B. and Hughes, M. (1984) *Young Children Learning,* London: Fontana.

Vygotsky, L. (1978) *Mind and Society: The Development of Higher Psychological Processes,* Cambridge, Mass.: MIT Press.

Vygotsky, L. (1986) *Thought and Language,* Cambridge, Mass.: MIT Press.

Wells, G. (1986) *The Meaning Makers,* London: Hodder and Stoughton.

Chapter 4

'But they're pink!' – 'Who cares!'
Popular culture in the primary years

Cathy Pompe

> Contemporary children's culture exists because merchandising interests are willing to invest in the production of children's television . . . there is ample evidence that the marketplace has been delivering 'what children want' better than any other contemporary agency of socialization.[1]

POGS

The deserted school library at the end of the day. I am dismantling a display of toys and merchandise some 9-year-olds had set up for their video interviews. From a distance two older unknown boys are circling around like sharks, silent and wary as drug dealers. Eventually somebody mediates for us: they want to buy my unopened box of *Pogs* from the display. *Pogs* are the little collectable discs of card with funny pictures on them which you buy from newsagents in surprise packs: you can swop your doubles and play dexterity/gambling games to win or lose them to your friends. There's a whole encyclopaedic knowledge about the different discs which fuels experts' conversations and confers businessman-like status on the *Pog* barons of the playground. They have American origins. They are good to hold and shuffle. Never advertised from on high, the cleverly positioned *Pogs* spread through the energetic word-of-mouth channels of a children-only under-culture. Many children have collected over 250 *Pogs* in past weeks, at £1 for six. Even the more sceptical consumers got hooked: 'I thought *Pogs* were just bits of cardboard that were stupid. Now I've got some I think they're really great.' Now there are none in the shops, the stakes have risen, people will do anything – hence the shady *Pog* dealers in the deserted library. A few weeks later, shops awash with *Pogs* again, the school bans the articles: £10 is found to have been handed over for a single *Pog*, children are stealing and fighting, the situation is quite out of hand.

'BATMAN FOREVER'

It's the last week of the school year, Darren is going to see *Batman Forever* within days of its release. He comes to it full of anticipation and with layers of knowledge. He has a good contextual knowledge of the film as a product: Saturday morning TV has run review features about the film, children's presenters have been to America to interview actors and directors, and in the studios other presenters are happily waving about the merchandise, to and fro-ing the gossip like the rest of the media: that it cost $60 million to make, the size of the sets, why a new actor has stepped into the shoes of Batman . . .

More privately, Darren has many registers set in motion by the experience. Batman is an old acquaintance. When he was 5 or 6 he was interested, then he went off it, and now at 9 he likes it again. He's seen the 1960 Batman-in-tights TV series, some of which he found boring, and the stylish and sombre Warner Bros animated series, which he likes. What new contemporary vision of Batman will be brought to life on the big screen? Darren has had a chance to savour several times over juicy clips from *Batman Forever* shown on the current McDonald's advert, as well as seeing other extracts and stills here and there. There is something dark and powerful conjured that he hopes will go deep. Most importantly of all, he knows that one of his favourite people, the actor Jim Carrey, is playing the Riddler, the manic and deranged villain of the film. Meeting the Riddler will be like meeting a new person you already love, unknown but rich with the ghosts of personas Jim Carrey has already given you: the Pet Detective in *Ace Ventura*, Stanley Ipkiss in *The Mask*.

Inside the cinema a fantastical Gotham City extends beyond the screen. Surrounded by larger-than-life sounds Batman plunges through immense shafts in the blue darkness, protective and beautiful. The illusion is complete and Darren can surrender himself utterly to it. He has had nightmares about monsters, but this darkness is thrilling and comfortable. He knows how it will end for the villains, though not enough for it to spoil the delicious twists of the plot. Back at school Darren told me it was the best film he'd seen since he was 5. When he was 5 it had been King Kong.

It was a unique experience, like the single live theatrical performance in ancestral times. Once it has run, this film will never be shown in the cinema again. How does Darren hold on to the experience? He knows that in a year there will be the video; it won't be the same total immersion, but he will be able to go over all the best bits lots of times. Meanwhile, he has cut out all the pictures he can find in the newspapers in the house. Newsagents sell the book of the film, a bargain sticker album for 65p – that only leaves 200 stickers to collect at 23p for six. Knowing Darren, laid back, streetwise, he's not going to go for that. His attic and cupboards are the repositories of all the toys and books that saw him through the various crazes he has been through in his life. Now *Batman Forever* can live inside him. He is perfecting his crazy Jim Carrey faces. He has decided he wants to be an actor.

LOSING THEIR HEARTS AND MINDS TO DISNEY

Most teachers I know worry about the culture children are growing up in today, and worry about their own role and relation to it: ignore, forewarn or embrace?

Many of my friends say children are getting harder to teach. The classroom, with its one or two rickety computers and dog-eared books, can be an arid environment compared with the thrills and spills on offer outside. Compare the richness of a child's two experiences: the instant but multilayered reading of a fast-cutting film like *Batman Forever* versus the laborious decoding, in a restless classroom, of printed pages in a fiction book you have never heard of. It is probably the experience of feeling sophisticated versus that of being on foreign territory. The one leaves you suffused; the other you'll shrug off without a further thought.

In olden days children coming to school might have had new worlds opened up to them which they had no way of coming upon otherwise: great stories, a knowledge of other fascinating times and places, things to thrill and dream of. Nowadays, all the magic seems to lie firmly *outside*, and what we have to offer does not stand a chance of even being tried out. We are fearful, not just for ourselves but for the children.

First, there is the thin diet we fear they might end up with. Because it has all the resources to find out, the entertainment industry knows best what touches children, while its prime goal is to make money. Writers like Bob Dixon[2] and Stephen Kline,[3] among others, scathingly document the marketing strategies that deliberately feed children unlasting pleasures, leaving them forever slightly dissatisfied and ready to move on to the next alluring product, be it the new video game or the next special effects blockbuster. Dixon analyses the fantasy and desire conveyor belt that shunts children from *Cinderella* via *Sparkle Eyes Barbie* and girls' magazines into the arms of the make-up and fashion market. Television cartoon series are devised and funded by toy manufacturers whose prime purpose is to sell character figures: judicious plot twists are calculated to necessitate the purchase of a whole new set of characters.[4] The proliferation of TV channels means smaller audiences, less money to spend per programme, no time to do more than pull out a sure-fire idea from the recipe book and make up for lack of detail in the animation with a lot of 'Kerpow!' Original ideas can't be taken up as they pose too much of a financial risk, so it's best to stick with 100 per cent good versus evil and manly killer hunts versus alluring but can't-run-in-the-jungle-in-her-high-heels blondes.

We worry that these undernourished children used to the short-lived buzz of enticing cultural products are falling into an addiction: instant fixes and disposable thrills. They zap channels and surf the net: it's the three minute culture. Do they have a memory? Are they losing the ability to concentrate? Are they frightened of silence? Do they still know the pleasure of making an effort and sticking with a challenging text or of opening themselves up to completely unfamiliar experiences? Have they switched off cognitive activity and gone into pure sensory stimulation mode? Are their imaginations impoverished by the minimal and repetitive narratives that catch their fancy? Are they losing the resources to find what would really nourish them, neglecting skills (like reading) that would open other doors and give them the powers they need?

We worry more than ever that it is David here and Goliath

out there. Disney, Mattel, Murdoch and Co. have the means to infiltrate our dreams, to place the *Pogs* at your newsagent's elbow just when you and your mates might have got into the mood for inventing a playground club or craze of your own. But the commercial product comes ready made and so attractive that it makes what you might have done seem shabby. You take one further step back from yourself as genius, and settle for yourself as consumer. But perhaps we can still tell and write our own stories and weave some magic in the classroom? But how does David 'write' or communicate in any way in the classroom that which is most vivid in his mind – some imagined rapid sequence of close-ups and sound-effects as his hero confronts the huge robot? Schools don't have the will or the technological resources required to empower children as writers of audio-visual texts. Are they, then, forever doomed to remain only consumers?

We also worry that too much is pouring into children's bedrooms on the crowded channels. The world has changed. There's child porn on the internet, snuff movies reputedly doing the rounds, and catchy tunes that 5-year-olds lap up turn out to have sexually explicit or criminal lyrics. The entertainment industry, going straight for our dreams of potency, is outdoing itself to bring ever more tension and killing onto the screen. The incidence of real disturbing things has probably not changed, but now it pours straight into children's lives, together with all the secrets that used to be the adults' preserve: real-life child murderers people children's imaginations, little boys know how rape goes and kids watch a lot of love-making. It must all be having some kind of effect. Many parents are fearful to let children go out of the house, torn between the need to protect them from what they might experience and the knowledge that children desperately need the space and freedom to find their own way. Because the grey side is all too much, the family smothers itself in lathers of reassuring Disney and plenty of tailor-made clean family fun from which all shadows have been clinically removed, no doubt creating in children's minds some overall cocktail of blancmange and toxic waste.

What do schools do? Do you create a bastion that keeps 'all that' out, so you can surround children with the texts and narratives they would not give themselves a chance to experience otherwise? How do you equip children with the resources to become aware of the cultural market of which they are a part, of the forces that determine what they get to read and see and want and do? How can we help them become 'more active and critical media users who will demand, and could contribute to, a greater range and diversity of media products'[5]? 'Exposing' the institutions that gave them more pleasure than you ever did will probably not get you very far. Or do you barge in with an enthusiastic let-me-in smile and gatecrash the out-of-school domains where children are busy nurturing private pleasures and knowledge, and their adult-resistant cultures and identities? How can you share children's references and pleasures when you're not up watching *Sonic the Hedgehog* at the crack of dawn on Saturday, you don't get the Nickelodeon channel, have never had a go on a mega drive, and probably don't even want to? And how can you possibly structure classroom learning experiences around material you know so little about?

WORKING IN SCHOOL – MY CONVICTIONS

To write this chapter I visited a school I am fond of, over a period of months, to see what I could find out about the popular culture experiences of a small bunch of 8–9-year-olds I was entrusted with. I wanted to see what kind of relationship we could strike up and where we could go with it. I came with many questions and uncertainties, but with a small baggage of convictions.

First, I take seriously the pleasures the children are deriving from their particular corners of the culture and believe they go deep, however tasteless they may appear to me. The culture out there is not in fact vacuous. Today's myth-makers know their onions. Some of the great story-tellers of our age are to be found working in the cinema. George Lucas and Steven Spielberg steeped themselves in ancient myths and erudite works[6] to find archetypes that would resonate with the spirit of our age, and created modern classics like *Star Wars* and *Jaws*. Further down the chain in amongst the junk there is lots of nourishment: it may be a low-budget watered-down animated Greek myth derivative in its hundredth recycling and drenched in Polly Pocket pink, but to the small child who comes across it for the first time in her life it might be a big moment. Our whole postmodern culture is a big hungry recycling machine, full of contradictions and complex feed loops. The comedy series of different decades, the artwork of far-away cultures, all are grist to the mill. Gritty myths that hit the spot for adults one year get dished out in low-budget kiddy form the next, still sparkling with the extra cachet. Advertising agencies with rarefied educational backgrounds produce stunning surrealist adverts that run past children many times over. Disney plunders non-Western cultures for new stories with which to colonize the world and alights on *Pocahontas*, a tale that denounces white imperialism. Plenty of rich matter there.

Second, it is not right to believe the entertainment industry dominates our culture simply because it imposes its products on us: critically, it does so because it has good means to find out what touches us, and to steal the best creative ideas where it finds them. Ultimately, the consumer and her desires have a lot of power. There is plenty of proof that the entertainment world is a hit and miss affair, with people falling over themselves to come up with products that will run, and losing money trying to copy a quirky success. After the *Teenage Mutant Ninja Turtles*, the brainchild of two unknown Americans, which drove young children berzerk in the early 1990s, there was a huge lull in that corner of the toy market. Bandai, the company that had marketed the Turtle toys, came up with several major new character ranges tied to potential hit media products (like *Little Dracula* and *Toxic Crusaders*), which sank without a trace. It was only several years later that Bandai found another winning formula with the *Mighty Morphin Power Rangers*, when a new generation of children who had not overdosed on 'Cowabunga!' were ready for a fresh round of martial arts hero adventures. On the whole I trust that when children have exhausted the personal nourishment in a cultural product (however short, long or expensive the process might be) they will discard it and not stay hooked like zombies. The short spans of attention we complain of in children perhaps signify a healthy response to low-nutrient products.

I also believe that, like the reader of written texts, the viewer is an active meaning maker. In amongst all the contradictory strands on the box there is a huge amount of space where 'readers' make their own meanings: the experience of zapping between an advert for an anorexic Sindy doll and a snatch of emaciated bodies on the news might set up trains of thought that are very different from the respective responses of 'I want to be like Sindy!' and 'the world is too horrible!', which an 'effects' model of television viewing would like us to believe.[7] In *Television, Sex Roles and Children* Durkin suggests that 'more viewing provides more scope for diversity', and that 'frequency is not equivalent to saliency'.[8] Through watching more TV you have in fact got a better chance of stumbling upon something completely different. A single counter-stereotypical message encountered might loom quite large in your mind, even set against the hundreds of other stereotype-reinforcing experiences you have had.

The world and children have indeed changed: children are exposed to a lot, but they are also protected and equipped by all their knowledge. Experienced viewers ride horror films like roller-coasters, shrieking but safe, because they know the narrative codes of the genre. They watch bullet-riddled villains crashing through the windows of high-rise office blocks with all the deconstructing knowledge they got from programmes like *How Do They Do That?* They know about modality and the syntax of films. The nature of their pleasures has undoubtedly changed somewhat, with gains and losses, but there is no going back.

Finally, I believe classrooms should be potent spaces in which children feel bubbly and confident, swept up in exciting topics and narratives that will engage hearts, touch funnybones, feed dreams, nourish imaginations and generally hit the spot. Then they might just want to play along with us and allow us to help unlock their potential. It's a partnership. Finding rich common grounds where children and teachers can live pleasurably together might take a lot of work. There are fraught relationships to heal between wounded teachers and resistant pupils. For the teacher, it might start with attuning a little to the culture children are nourished by, finding opportunities to mess around pleasurably in informal spaces with them, on equal terms, sharing things they are prepared to tell you, asking light questions that are deeply clear of any judgemental or instructional intent. It might even involve sinking into the plush seat of a cinema to watch something you would never have chosen to see and letting yourself feel like a child again, or permitting yourself to watch some real garbage on the box and be horrified that you enjoyed it.

WORKING IN SCHOOL – A TRIPOD, A CAMERA AND A SUITCASE OF GARISH MAGAZINES

The large primary school I visited is set in the middle of a council estate to the north of Cambridge. Initially I came in one morning a week to work with six 8–10-year-olds. Over a term and a half we moved from informal discussions and the sharing of favourite bits of video to the creation of their own short video magazine for 7–10-year-olds, 'Cheesy Feet'. This involved interviewing other children, doing surveys, writing stories, creating trailers for their own blockbusters, and all sorts. In the last week of the school year I came in every day, we had the spacious school library as a base, their ideas took wing and we opened up to the input of children from other classes, who added new voices and energy to our work. As I write, 'Cheesy Feet' is still in production. While I was in the school I interviewed at length all but one of the seven junior teachers: two of them introduced me to specific pupils whom I worked with for a little. I also interviewed the parents of three children in their homes.

Picture four 8-year-olds: Peter, a quiet boy whose earnest thoughts often didn't hit the table fast enough to get a full hearing; David, an ardent soul but suppressed by his own low self-opinion; Kerry, unconfident but most generous in spirit; Martine, who has a cosy energy but holds back from testing the limits. For added zest I took up the further offers of Jason, 8, a bit of a loner, lithe, guarded and streetwise, who became strongly committed to the project, and Aisha, a 9-year-old from the same class, a great leader of minds with scatty overtones. Later on we also drew in 9-year-old Darren, fair, quiet and easy, to boost our internal dynamics. Several of these children do not have easy home lives. We started as a tight group and fragmented into different combinations of teams as I tried to find the best ways to bring out the different voices.

Establishing relationships with the children was a delicate affair. I hoped for a degree of openness and trust, and I was in fact fairly well placed to find it. The children called me by my first name and I cut a glamorous figure by virtue of the tripod and camcorder I carried about. My suitcase of toy catalogues and magazines (from *Mighty Max* to *Just Seventeen*) hypnotized all who saw it, and untangling microphones and audio equipment gave our work an important and pleasurable aura even when nothing special was going on. The teachers had generously put me under no pressure to achieve an end result, and we had cosy times hanging around together. At home I watched the films and programmes they talked about. For the children it was festively free of the 'now write about it' catch which surrounds some of the treats we offer them in school. The festive space had its own deep but slow dynamics. I refrained from exercising teacherly powers, because it would have closed important doors and swamped the process with my own agenda. Looking for ways to approach them, waiting for children's own voices and desires to come through, was a desperately slow process. In the end my own concerns inevitably dripped through: the questions I had asked them were picked up and re-used when they conducted their own interviews with other children – children are highly absorbent. All in all, they were astute and impassioned in their informal comments but almost completely powerless when it came to harnessing their skills and taking charge, and bringing to realization any project that was in several stages. There was a critical breakdown point on the border between freedom and spontaneity (the place where they feel most themselves) and school work and effort (where they are usually working to someone else's agenda). However, as 'Cheesy Feet' took off, I crept into the position, in my capacity as producer, where I could bully them into some hard work without trampling on their emerging ideas and wishes.

Most of the time I was there I was full of misgivings and depressed about how hard it was to make something happen, yet now I feel very rich. The insights I have gathered over the months do not have the status of rigorous research nor did they give me answers to many questions. At no point were the children able to express in words what the Mighty Morphin Power Rangers really did for them, and my discrete analytical leading questions were mostly like water off a duck's back. The elaborate working environment we created was there to catch a wealth of odd moments where something unexpected or genuine seemed to come up. Take the sneering comment of an angry 7-year-old: 'I don't like Superman: he thinks he's so smart he's broken his neck!' (Christopher Reeves, the actor who had played Superman, had recently tragically been paralysed in a riding accident.) Or there is the moment when Aisha hovered about after school and asked to make a quick videobox statement about Pamela Anderson (the blonde bombshell of *Baywatch* fame): 'I don't like Pamela Anderson [holding up pin-up]. I think she's a sexy wexy, another girl who wants to start diabetes [for diabetes read anorexia]. I think she was very good in *Baywatch* but I don't like her at all.' I had previously questioned Aisha about the Little Mermaid's scant bikini, which she had fully endorsed ('I think she's fine . . . she'd look silly in a T-shirt'). Somewhere happily beyond my reach Aisha's own views about women in scant bikinis are shaping themselves.

WORKING IN SCHOOL

Carnival

Most striking was the seduction and appeal, the electric energy unleashed by the 'popular culture' items I wheeled into school. Disney, *Gamesmaster* and *Littlest Pet Shop* represented all that was joyful. One teacher commented on the difficulty of bringing up popular culture references in the classroom: it is often simply too explosive to handle. 'You mention Power Rangers and the next day you're snowed under with 200 figures.' I was myself always popular simply for carrying around a few Batman figures and Sindy dolls ('You do such interesting things Cathy!'): frenzied children in the playground squashed their noses against the windows of the library where we worked among mouth-watering plastic treasures. Of course, part of the appeal lies with the deliciously school-free connotations of these items, which we would undoubtedly ruin if we drew them into the curriculum. Then again, some of the glamour is simply to be read on the price tag: teachers are quick to point out the consumer one-upmanship of the culture, another difficulty to negotiate when referring to it in the classroom (bring on the child who always has twice as many of whatever as anybody else). However, some of the appeal surely lies in the playful and accessible nature of these items: they are saturated with the children's experiences of friendly interactions and of feeling in control. Primary classrooms are quick to banish playing beyond the infant years, yet at home juniors still watch TV programmes while they play with all the relevant figures on the carpet. *Girl Talk* is full of things to do, cut out and send off. The *My Little Mermaid* magazine, even for the poor reader, is full of decodable meanings connected to the vivid experience of seeing the film and TV programmes.

Finally the glamour associated with our work didn't only lie in the popular culture 'texts' we were handling: the video camera was an important friend to the children, giving them a voice, putting them in touch with a potential audience they could believe in, through a medium that they fully appreciate and which dominates their lives, an expertise which school pretty much sidelines. The electricity surrounding such a presence in the school speaks of fresh hopes of potency awakened. A teacher friend pointed out to me how bringing audio-visual work into the classroom can sometimes destabilize the quiet hierarchies of the classroom: suddenly the kingpins of the traditional literacy are toppled as a different set of children, previously disempowered, come into their own.

'I like *Power Rangers* because it shows you how to save the world'

One of the most interesting dimensions of this project was probing the multi-level personalities the children operate in and out of. One moment the children were slavering over some juicy bit of gore they'd relished; the next they were denouncing with sanctimonious 'internalized parent' voices the fact that small children shouldn't watch *Power Rangers* because it would lead them to go out and kill each other. Just like the illusion that the researcher can observe a situation without influencing it, the fact that children say and mean different things in different situations and in front of different people cautions against a simplistic interpretation of their utterances. The phenomenon of multilayered response is well documented. In *Children and Television*[9] Hodge and Tripp give very full descriptions of their research situations and analyse the markers that distinguish the different 'kinds of self' that children speak from. They suggest that 'child-utterances', the hedonistic, subversive and amoral points of view, are characterized by 'loudness or energy, rising or falling intonation, and the presence of laughter' (p. 48). The opposite typically marks 'parent-discourse', the internalized voice of an authority figure. In *Children Talking Television*[10] David Buckingham analyses in further great detail the complex social and other dynamics of what children say to adults and in front of each other.

As I hinted before, children are highly sensitive and receptive, and they learn to say what they think you want to hear. When I asked her about any reservations she might have about *The Little Mermaid*, Aisha quickly came up with a line she thought would do: 'It could be dangerous, because little children might go in the water and drown.' When we got free tickets for a screening of Disney's 1995 animation *Pocahontas* months before its general release, I leapt at the chance to explore subtly – as I thought – their awareness of the workings of the Disney empire. To my casual question 'Why does Disney make good movies?', Jason vehemently launched into a garbled denunciation, beating several others to it: 'Ah, because they're so rich and they're trying to make millions of money [etc., etc.].' Despite his fervour, it was so neat and dutifully delivered that I couldn't help suspecting that he was picking up on some patter he must have heard from a teacher at some point. Even more splendid was Jason's response when, in an impromptu and inspired *Oprah* show, Aisha got to him and asked what he would do to improve the *Power Rangers* programmes: 'More girls', he echoed implausibly, with a kind of neutral smarminess. The teachers also documented the discrepancy between what children will say in class and what they carry on doing and thinking outside. Talking about her attempts to shake the deadly grip of the status conferred by material possessions, one teacher joked: 'They'll say all the right things, give out corny lines like "it's not what you have that matters it's who you are", then coolly carry on with their ugly confrontations in the playground.'

It was clear that the deepest issues were always going to be alluded to obliquely. They might be impossibly hard to express in words: consider the inadequacy of this pat response from a little girl who was working with me in a one-off session: 'I like *Power Rangers* because it shows you how to save the world!' Sometimes things may be too important to talk about in the open. In an intimate moment, Tina worked her way round to telling me how she had one day finally thrown all her My Little Ponies in the dustbin, following her mum's going on about her being too old to play with them. A few days later she was more safely referring to the incident as the time she 'gave away' all her Ponies.

SOME INSIGHTS – PROTECTIVE DEVICES

The multiple voices with which children speak are in fact heartening: I gained a healthy impression of children's inner resources: there were many different voices playing in their heads, a lot more sloshing around then we might suspect. Terminators and fluffy bunnies happily coexist within, providing children the balance of hard and soft, shelter and exposure, which they need to give themselves, like Alice in Wonderland nibbling at the mushroom. The children bracing themselves to watch the horror video *Child's Play* also sneak in doses of *Sesame Street* and *Babar*. Boys playing with Action Man keep an eye on Sindy and Polly Pocket from afar. In the frenetic culture there is a great complexity of voices children are hearing. In Aisha, a fascination with *Interview with the Vampire* ('It's not fair the girl who plays in it is 14 and we're not allowed to see it till we're 18!') and *Congo* happily coexisted with an appetite for the most inane jokes. When I asked Stephen what multi-million-dollar blockbuster he would like to see being made, he first came up with plans for a new 'Freddy' (*Nightmare on Elm Street*) horror film (cert. 18), but then pulled something quite different out of his hat: his storyboard was a variation on *Casper*, the cosy ghost film about to be released. Talking to him later, I found *Street Fighter* and *Judge Dredd* jostling with *Monty Python and the Holy Grail*: (excited tones) 'There's this guy, King Arthur, was looking for some knights and he didn't have a horse so he was just clapping these coconuts as he went along!' It was he and Philip, telling stories on video with an eclectic selection of the character toys I had put out, who provide the unforgettable dialogue:

Philip (fearing his character has been written off):   Am I still in it?'

Stephen, alias Cyborg-Batman (urgently):   Get your person! We're going to Batman Castle, 'cos we need to get my magic slippers [grabs My Little Mermaid's plastic shoes].

Philip: But they're pink!
Stephen (recklessly):   Who cares!

When Aisha carried out a class survey of favourite TV programmes (probably conducted with power-trip officiousness
and with the children checking for previous popular responses),
it threw up *Neighbours* and co., the old soap opera standards.
Yet soaps never came up in our group. I came to the school
at the height of the *Mighty Morphin Power Rangers* craze: the
programme and toys elicited the greatest reverence and desire
in some, and even the children least drawn in kept abreast of
developments as a high priority. Yet, when as a group we picked
programmes to record and watch snippets of in future sessions,
a whole range of cosy, humorous programmes emerged as firm
favourites: there was the absurd slapstick and mime programme
called *ZZap*; the cartoon *Animaniacs*, a kind of Marx Brothers
meets Mickey Mouse; *Rugrats*, an American cartoon charting the
drama in the everyday lives of a bunch of precocious toddlers (a
kind of *Peanuts* for the 1990s); *Clarissa Explains it All*, sit-com
type lessons in life from a strong and likeable young American
teenage girl, with a good sense of humour. Top of the children's
charts was the splendidly repulsive *Mr Bean*, the comic anti-
hero created by Rowan Atkinson. Altogether it's hardly a viewing range to fuel the worry that children fed on popular culture
will metamorphose into Rambo and Barbie. From the wide
range of films on video which were available to us to dip into,
the children elected to watch snippets from *Mrs Doubtfire*, the
film adaptation of the novel by the British children's writer
Anne Fine, a drama about a divorced father dressing up as a
middle-aged female housekeeper so that he gets to spend time
with his estranged children. The film is enhanced by the comic
performance of the actor Robin Williams, but it steers resolutely
clear of a saccharine ending and the children's parents never
get back together again.

Listening to the children watching a chunk of *Power Rangers*
and an episode of *Mr Bean* I was astonished at the interactive
quality of *Mr Bean* compared with the absorbed silence of
watching *Power Rangers*: viewing *Mr Bean* was peppered with
laughter, squeals and excited predictions as the plot buckled
unpredictably from under their delighted expectations. In total
contrast, the act of participating in the soon-to-be-tired-of but

for now still deeply thrilling re-enactment of 'Morphing Time!', followed by the Power Rangers' ritual confrontation and inexorable defeat of the enemy, was an almost religious experience for some. The two viewing experiences were nourishing different parts of themselves. There still seems to be a rich menu to dip into out there, with different valuable nutrients on offer and children helping themselves to a varied range. The one-programme-a-week regime (e.g. you can only watch *The Animals of Farthing Wood*) offered by some parents who fear the contamination of popular culture in their children's lives may not be addressing their nutritional needs in the best way. I document further on that some of the children with big appetites for 'popular culture' were also developing voracious appetites for reading and for inputs of all varieties. There is no reason why a fixation on *Puppy in my Pocket* can't grow alongside a taste for Philippa Pearce – in fact, any such newcomer to *A Dog so Small* would probably feel very welcome. One of the teachers, who saw a role for herself in helping pupils put their popular culture obsessions into perspective, was in fact most worried about the child from a protective family who had never allowed herself to develop any appetites at all. To develop the cafeteria metaphor I feed in Bazalgette and Buckingham's[11] point that TV is one of the media where children have most control over what they experience: which films, videos and even books they have access to is often mediated by parents and other adults.

The children had a sizeable latent baggage of programmes they carried in corners of their minds, through living with older or younger children and adults. As confirmed in the literature, much of their viewing consisted of adult/general TV. When they trailed about in drapes and feathers for the jokes feature in their video 'Cheesy Feet', Aisha and Kerry suddenly realized they looked 'old-fashioned' and promptly donned French accents ('we're caught up in the war in France!') to declaim: 'Long ago in the year 1992 . . .' Their historical precision may have been way adrift, but they showed a genuine groping for knowledge and a fascination for other times and places. These two girls have their eyes open to the world in its many forms: they are certainly not content to be locked in Barbie-land or *Baywatch*. Their interest will be fed by sources as varied as the school history books that might come their way or the Catherine Cookson TV adaptations they've told me they watch. A year 6 teacher adamantly claimed that, for all the materialism and garish pinks of today's culture, his pupils had a bigger imagination that those same children would have had thirty or forty years ago: they had a wide knowledge to draw on. To take just one example, their heads were full of strange and challenging imagery from the abstract and surreal language of pop videos.

Again, just as children can make themselves impermeable to schooling, they seem to shut out what's on the box when they need to, or to negotiate it. David Morley[12] among others documents the varied ways people interact with the TV set in the corner. Here he quotes an interviewee: 'a lot of the time the programme will actually spark off the discussion. We turn it down so we are watching it *and* having a discussion at the same time.' In the families I visited things seemed pretty integrated, with television important but far from tyrannical. All the children had been allowed to be totally engrossed by TV at various stages, and they had been given lots of toys in honour of their particular infatuations, but they seemed to have worked their way through it and at this point they could happily take it or leave it. Tina apparently never put TV before her friends, though her mother feared she might get addicted to soaps, as she herself was! Darren's family had deliberately cut back on the amount of viewing they did together because they found there was too little time in life: Darren, among others, was a big talker who needed an attentive audience. Darren did occasionally see 18 certificate videos in friends' houses, but his parents were secure that he could shield himself from traumatic experiences. Peter's more protective family played a lot of traditional games together, though they also often treated themselves to a real family 'cinema' experience in the living room, with curtains drawn and nibbles at hand. As summer arrived, I found television generally receded in children's preoccupations. A teacher reported that, worried by her impression that children did nothing but watch the box all day, she had done a survey of pupils' lives outside school: she had been astonished by the wide range of activities and interactions they all seemed to be involved in, from Brownies to chess, karate and cycling. Even watching short snippets of video in the group, I found children eager to get on with something different after a while.

The things children watch are put into perspective by the other things they watch or know about, and by their many other interactions with books, friends, and life. Their many-compartmented minds make for new kinds of multilayered and deconstructed pleasures, which offer a measure of switch-on switch-off protection and detachment. Impressions do not drop into still clear pools, as we like to imagine they did in a bygone age.[13] Children know an actor is leaving the soap and can regulate to some extent the pain they experience in the screen death of the character involved.[14] They know the codes of television genres: these amiable baddies won't die because the audience has identified with them too much, while these cardboard cut-out villains are ripe for an enjoyable despatch. As one teacher put it, children brazenly enjoy McDonald's burgers in full and cynical awareness of the state of the rainforests. They have a survivor's way of plucking pleasures and nourishment from the experiences offered to them, while being able to open or close other attendant compartments in their minds.

Work with the children yielded much evidence that children lap up specific items in the culture which nourish them and shrug off the rest (or store it in a different place). The age group straddles a spectrum which runs from playing with dolls and figures to play-acting with *Just Seventeen*, and from the fantasies of *He-Man* and co. to the starker realism of football. I found children of the same age at completely different stages, living in distinct worlds created by their own tastes and choices. Picture Aisha and Kerry in the nurse's room, developing an idea for 'Cheesy Feet'. They are pretending to lie on bunk beds, the item is called 'Gossip':

Aisha-in-role (dreamily):   Guess what! I've asked this boy out! Oh my God, I didn't mean to!
[Stony silence]
Aisha-director (peering to bunk below):   Kerry, it's your turn, you have to say: 'You never guess what I done!'
[Kerry squirms in the bunk below]
Kerry: I don't want to. [swinging from the bed frame and changing the subject] Me, I'm a monkey.

Growing out of things

Teachers reported how their own offspring had emerged unscathed from various 'tasteless' addictions and how, for them,

TV had not squeezed out books. One eloquently asserted her confidence that children are nourished by and grow out of their fixations. After a couple of cycles they see the past and future stretching out away 'from the toys strewn on the floor which were last year's passion'. Unlike some of her colleagues, she was adamant that children will not choose endless rubbish. She described how the infant who brought a *He-Man* book into school loved the pictures but wouldn't in fact sit out a full reading of the *He-Man* text if it was offered to him. She contrasted that with the powerful hold she knew other classroom storybooks could exercise over that same child.

SOME INSIGHTS – CHILDREN SURFING THE WAVES

Children's vulnerabilities

There is an interplay between children's propensity to subvert, send up, debunk and resist those things which have power over them, and their vulnerability and allegiance to the things that have caught their fancy. Children's playfulness, their being game for anything is also a vulnerability. Aisha looking through the *Radio Times* gasped, 'Oh, excellent!' at every turn, and the children routinely gave programmes ten out of ten, the more recent the better. They are ready to play with anyone who is willing to get them going, manufacturers and teachers alike: one suggestion or one little prop dangled at them and they're off toying with a new scheme. They repeat what they're told, even the half-baked stuff, and laugh at jokes they don't understand. The manufacturers know how they play: children are charmed by all the little collectables and special tokens that drop out of packages, and manufacturers create the phoney specialist knowledge and rituals of expertise that whip up allegiance for a product. My children routinely subjected their interviewees to intimidating tests of knowledge, got them to recite the *Power Ranger* catechism and give other displays of cultural proficiency ('How many *Pogs* are there in Series 2?'). These children also fell straight for the calculated shifts of manufacturers: Aisha, the first to announce the demise of her interest in *Power Rangers*, bounced in many weeks later: 'I've changed my mind about *Power Rangers*: I think it's excellent! They've dumped Rita [the arch villain] and they've got this utterly different man! This one is a lot more lethal!'

Informal channels of information

I was impressed by the way they worked all the different informal network systems to find out what was going on in the culture at large. With their own formal literacy skills not in full operational mode, and seemingly no very clear sense of time, they nevertheless operated like shrewd business people running a complex operation, every school corridor an information-gathering opportunity, every adult conversation a possible lead. They did not use TV programme schedules nor did they particularly timetable their lives, but somehow they found out what was on. I also found them very sensitive to all the vibes and messages travelling along the grapevine: what was hot to whom, what was a waste of time. 'Michael Jackson's £25 new CD with loads of his old songs is a rip off!' – Aisha passes this on to us as we work. When we compiled a list of films both old and brand new, David was leading us at every turn. Yet when we went to *Pocahontas* I discovered that he had never been to the cinema in his life and many of the films he knew all about were many months from ever coming out on video.

Guys and dolls

Aspects of the popular culture industry, like the toy industry, present a tableau dramatically divided along gender lines. There was plenty of evidence of the tyranny exerted, the pressure to conform and what one teacher called the 'fear of the middle ground'. You can't find red sandals for a 3-year-old, one teacher illustrates. In their interviews the power-hungry video-makers (who made their interviewing situations as formal and intimidating as possible) went straight for the cut and dried questions like asking boys whether they played with girls' toys and vice versa, to which the cornered interviewees dished up implacably correct and unrevealing answers. Teachers and parents also spoke to me about the many other pressures to conform, with regard to clothing (the need to have the proper expensive shoes), about the way status was linked to possessions ('the child who's got X is top dog') and the vulnerability and desperation of the less secure children.

RESISTANCE AND NEGOTIATING DEVICES

Debunk and resist

Anarchy and humour are children's best protective and subversive devices, with which they upturn the most intimidating sacred icons and declare their grasp of what's going on, usually well out of our hearing, and at the drop of a hat.[15] Fresh out of the film *Pocahontas*, with *Pogs* still all the rage in school, Aisha decided 'Cheesy Feet' needed a story called 'Pog-a-Hontas'. In a quick moment in front of the camera a dressed-up Marlon (friendly classmate aged 9) performed a terse and surreal sequence in the style of 'How to Make a Fur Coat', deftly mocking himself, posh accents and silly TV programmes in one fell swoop. Humour is the ground on which children feel comfortable and powerful. The first solid ground the children found for 'Cheesy Feet' to develop from was the jokes department, and playful silliness was the territory where the least resourceful of the children finally found the energy and confidence to express themselves. The group loved Channel 4's zany *Big Breakfast*,[16] and the programmes they identified as important to them all contained a mixture of the cosy and the liberating.

Playfulness, and the confidence to be playful, is the quality that marked out the children who seemed to stand open to influence but free. Here are two children I got to know a little better than some.

Tina, 10, and from a different class, is a remarkable free spirit. She follows in the footsteps of her mother, erstwhile tomboy and voracious Mills and Boon reader, and she has a prolific imagination. All is grist to the mill, the pace is fast.

Ariel (handing over the baby to the Red Power Ranger):   Here you are, you hold her. You can look after her for a little while. [Baby cries]
Red Ranger: Oh dear she's done a poo now. I'll have to change her nappy.
[He is swiftly interrupted by the Power Ranger Theme Tune: 'Go, go, Power Rangers!']

Red Ranger (speaking through intercom with American accent):   Yes Zordon? Come in [Inaudible reply]. I'm busy . . . OK beam me up.
Pink Power Ranger: I thought you'd never come!

When I asked Tina's mother how Tina might have developed her flexibility and imagination, she cast around and mentioned the way she would get Tina to see different shapes inside clouds in the sky when she was very small. In Tina's mother I had a powerful impression of someone determined to open big windows to look out from, from inside a constrained life, surrounded on the whole by people more conventional than herself. Tina and her mother apparently also really know how to have fun: they give themselves days seriously devoted to pleasure, like delicious trips to Alton Towers.

Tina is very much her own person. She has a sound knowledge of cultural icons and she wheels them in and out of the theatre of her mind with complete ease. She is herself now a voracious reader. When she was in the infants' school Disney's *Little Mermaid* came out and struck the deepest of chords in her. It stays with her still. She plays for hours with figures and sings with a strong voice lyrics to go with her often romantic narratives. She has an Aladdin-and-Jasmine duvet on her bed and suitcases full of glittering Barbies in wonderful outfits. She also borrows her brother's male character toys. Why doesn't she have her own? Her mother thinks it's a bit silly to buy a girl boys' toys, but if she were a *Home Alone* person she'd buy *Action Man, Power Rangers, Jurassic Park* stuff and lots of boys' videos. 'If I was living in my own house I'd play with all the babyish stuff, and with boys' stuff.' She reports the taunts of friends and the various pressures to jettison her *My Little Pony* collection etc., now water under the bridge: 'Dolls are babyish!', Aisha's 7-year-old little sister tells her. 'You play with your brother's toys!', denounces Martine. Tina's determination to honour her need to play is perhaps a clue to her power: she has ridden all the best narratives till they are hers to twist and turn at will and project her voice into. In Tina's stories girls are often still victims, but you feel she has things under control – at any moment she may authorize a major upheaval in the narrative codes. In her school storybook there is an intriguing story written in the first person, where she allows minor undignified pranks to be played on herself (e.g. spider tricks) and gives the boy character the fun role and all the good lines. Yet she undeniably remains the director who controls and brings to life all these characters, and she knows she can annihilate them with the same creative sweep. Like the flexible reed versus the brittle oak tree of the fable, the story-teller willing to inhabit the grotty parts probably has more power than the fragile egos who are playing out *Rambo* all day long.

Darren, who went to see *Batman Forever* at the beginning of this chapter, is also in the process of developing his own brand of counter-cultural voice to run alongside the various male personas he presents to the world every day. Darren is just about out of playing with figures and out of the grip of fantasy adventures. He is not planning a wholesale move into football. To stay cool in the relevant circles he has to present a slightly scruffy appearance. But he has always sided with underdogs and has friendships with children who stand outside the norm. His stories are now full of earnest jungle exploration adventures. In *Batman Forever* his favourite character remains the equally earnest adolescent role-model Robin. However, Jim Carrey, the Riddler and free spirit, is feeding him another line, a potent new persona to try out, one in a line of ridiculous-but-strong comic male figures to whom his older brothers have introduced him: John Cleese, Harry Enfield, *Mr Bean*, and so on. They lend him new wings to try out in private and lay further foundations for Darren the comedian, a character that has so far probably only fully come out in the intimacy of home, where he has long known how to make his family fall about with laughter.

WHAT SCHOOL CAN DO

Powerful places

School is a powerful institution at the service of children. Parents I spoke to attested to the formative roles it had played, to the impact of project work. *The Demon Headmaster* by Gillian Cross, which had recently been read in class, was echoing in their minds when my little group started on their first video drama, which they called 'The Demon Kidnapper'. I witnessed the continuing ripples from an earlier advertising project and the drip drip of my own ideas. School has the means to channel and mobilize children's faculties, so that they can see through certain explorations that will give them a sense of their own powers in a way they may never experience elsewhere. Assisted by the full drumming-up powers of the curriculum and honoured with serious curriculum time, we might have eased Aisha, the director of 'Cheesy Feet', into forms of personal organization that would have made her realize what she could really do, and mobilize the powerful woman lurking within.

All the teachers I spoke to acknowledged the importance of the culture 'out there'. They all had ways of relating to it, though most felt that what they did was not enough. Some were attentive to the informal discourse at playtime and made time to be open to the confidences of children then. Others felt aware of the school as a site where alternative messages stand a chance of being heard and where children might be put through some awareness-raising experiences: one street-wise year 6 teacher, fully aware of the subtle interplay between the cultures meeting in school, would nevertheless periodically organize to come down like a ton of bricks and do his Sindy rant and rave. Both he and others were aware of the oppositional role teachers have to play when fads and cultural icons are subversive markers of subcultures and of child identities. 'If I started to take these things too seriously they wouldn't quite know how to handle it.' The teacher speaking here has developed a provocative relationship of 'interested mockery' which she feels her fourth and fifth years can handle. 'They say, "I've got 300 *Pogs*", and I say, "You've got a problem!".' She has her own easy touch underpinned by working-class roots and will make a humorous display of revulsion on perusing some pink and plastic horror submitted for her inspection, before asking aghast: 'You sit at home and play with *this*!' She would affectionately denounce as 'saddies' a self-conscious classroom gang who were going through a long phase of collectively wearing black, by her reaction in fact fuelling the stance they were making. Ironic comments now pass to and fro, the class seems awash with subcultures, plane-spotters and 'anoraks'. With her own briefcase plastered with *Star Trek* stickers she is of course fair game for their teases: 'Sad, sad, Trekkie!' While she is trying to get children to laugh at themselves, she is in fact skilfully establishing a critical platform for diversity in her class. And, amidst the humorous banter, she is sowing seeds about the kinds of cultural experiences she would also like them to have.

Schools as a site for critical thinking: pitfalls and opportunities

From the promised Sindy rant in year 6 to perceived opportunities to study the culture industries under the heading of 'economic awareness', schools can offer children opportunities to reflect critically. Systematically learning to enquire about who made a cultural product, who is communicating, how we found out about it, how it reached us, is (some of) the stuff of media education.[17] A frank look at economics, at the toy and media industries and their mechanisms, down to chronicling, in as full and accurate detail as possible, the orchestrated launch of media products, can draw on children's detective skills in the up-to-the-minute culture. Training on quite fascinating and glamorous subject matter ('Jim Carrey is in Florida doing the new *Ace Ventura* movie!') the potentially formidable and impartial powers which serious curriculum time can offer, children can get deeply interested in collecting and organizing information in rigorous and fascinating ways, all the while drawing on subject matter that is ringing lots of bells for them and is plentiful. Some of it will be stored in compartments in their minds until a time when they might be ready to draw conclusion or insight from it. These are things teachers can teach 'upfront' if need be, in the manner of the Sindy rant; or they could also be explored through simulations and production work, where children can develop a pretty shrewd awareness and understanding of the working of the culture industry without being required to rail against institutions they might feel quite friendly towards.

However, the potent critical faculties which we know children already have, the explosive debunking resources, which we would like to call into play in relation to the culture, are very deep-seated. They probably reside somewhere in the same inalienable place as their perceptions that a lot of school is a waste of time, and other controversial insights they usually keep to themselves. Simply handing over critical tools and strategies to children is liable to jerk them back into a subservient automatic-pilot compliance which won't reach very deep.

Witness Aisha's grumpy response to my asking her for the results of her survey of people's favourite TV, which went something like: 'Oh don't bother me now, anyway, yeah, I know who won.' It reveals her assumption that there was some kind of pre-ordained right answer in this teacher-imposed activity, which in my naive perception had started out as a mutually agreed investigation, but from which the real Aisha had at some point decamped. To mobilize the full Aisha I suspect we have to take a messier route, which draws us further in and threatens to rewrite the agenda of the classroom.

Eat your heart out, Batman

If we want a stake in the battle for the attention of children I don't think we can afford to keep sheltered, harmonious and coy, waving a counter-cultural diet of improving and wholesome texts, and offering admittance to a beautiful high culture swathed in nourishing silence. We need to rock them with the best and grittiest we have to offer, multilayered narratives which make them feel clever and touch raw nerves, and which do disconcerting double takes on Disney. Children's author Robert Swindells has courted controversy with a book like *Stone Cold*, but his writing is devoured by children. We have to let children see that we too carry with us our very own friendly jam-packed and many-compartmented virtual suitcases, crammed with different voices, stories, escaping music, and useful objects to cover every eventuality. Let us not transport them to hallowed marbled silences they have no comfortable associations with. To me, Michael Rosen is the model here for the adult who knows how to nourish the playful child within; and consequently he becomes a resource to children, cultivating in them an irreverent and voracious appetite for paper pleasures (from Homer to telephone directories) to rival the huge and eclectic screen appetites of children.

We have also to descend by ourselves into some of the worlds our pupils inhabit – the virtual, the jagged and the bland – and in the safety of our own private playgrounds (finger on the rewind button of the video maybe) try to find inside us personas that might resonate from afar with the fantasies and concerns of pupils and which might help us beat a path to the place where they might come alive in our presence.

Children are getting harder to teach, and they need to be. They are endlessly manipulated, and persuaded into doing slightly alienating things, from buying *Pogs* to being dragged along a classroom scheme which sometimes only makes complete sense when you're standing where the teacher is. (Witness David in the first stages of 'Cheesy Feet', with the whole world at our feet: 'We could do a survey of favourite colours!' Dear David, aged 9, are you really and truly interested in finding out what people's favourite colours are? Or are you so used to tasks that feel grinding and meaningless to you that a feeble investigation like this looks to you like quite a cosy option?) If we don't want to be left with children whose hearts and minds have taken the exit door, we need to let them guide us to the kinds of places where they feel involved, clever and alert. However catalytic or oppositional the teacher's role might need to be on the job, it needs to be secretly guided by empathy within and ultimately stay open to the possibility that at any moment we might turn a corner and suddenly find ourselves opposite a child who is willing to say something to us from a very real place.

As teachers we have allowed ourselves to be burdened with an increasingly earnest and accountable top-down curriculum, set in stone, while we have let Murdoch and Disney, like Pied Pipers, steal the hearts of children and monopolize pleasure. We have banished play from school and are selling the children to toy multinationals who are leading a merry trail of buy, buy buy. There must be an alternative. I think it involves addressing several important areas.

Retreating to more solid ground

I believe schools need to nurture a culture where children are better able to be themselves. 'What's grey and has seventeen legs? An elephant on rollerblades.' Kerry falls about laughing. Except, of course, that she was supposed to have said, 'What's grey and has sixteen wheels?' Like the other conforming pressures we worry about outside, we ourselves participate in churning out children who are befuddled, clammed up, repeat what they think is right and are frightened of being laughed at. To take a step back to something they can feel playful towards, and experience a mastery of, to be allowed to operate from that strong place till they can really *roar*, follows the Tina-who-still-plays-with-dolls model. But it does not, of course, look impressive in the school records. Yet the price/prize being fought over is the right to grow up feeling potent and resourceful and live a life where, on the whole, you enjoy being yourself. With all the small group attention Kerry had received over the months we worked together it was only in the last days of 'Cheesy Feet', in the inviting space of the library, that she was gradually drawn to attire herself in lovely drapes and feathers and put on a silly pair of spectacles. Kerry as her very own person unfolded in front of me for the first time. Lounging on the sofa, a delicious blend of agony aunt and courtesan, she held forth carelessly and with some power: 'I am the Queen of Chadderwick! I rule this land! I like doing boogie boogie. I am the fairest of them all.' A modest start, perhaps, but a breeding ground for confidence once the voice of the carefree Kerry is validated and woven into the curriculum. It's a big shift in the agenda to take the curriculum closer to their powerful selves. It's a challenge to create class journeys where people offer each other enough space and acceptance so all can find and make places where they feel daring, contented and energized.

We probably all grow up too quickly, pressurized into jettisoning playful props and behaviours with which we were negotiating the outside world and making it our own. Playing spaces are probably the critical environments where we develop resources for survival: a grounded and pleasurable sense of self, the experience of potency, spontaneity and energy, and autonomy. Playfulness in school, which is so often abruptly halted at the doors of the junior school, vanishes into private underworlds and into the invigorating but callous open playing grounds of the entertainment culture. It is often there that young people will have the strongest experiences of feeling themselves: relaxed, spontaneous, unafraid. In disappearing from school, playfulness took with it the opportunities for personal projection and identification, the negotiating space where anything could be made to happen, which used to make the curriculum friendly and resonant. In the school where I hold a regular job, teachers have started reclaiming the ground surrendered to *Polly Pocket* and *Action Man* by infiltrating the curriculum with storyboxes, the powerful idea of Annabelle Dixon.[18] They are pleasurable home-made concoctions of play figures and assorted props designed to inspire and negotiate narratives, kept in boxes for children to take out when they want to launch into narrative mode. Storyboxes have opened story-telling floodgates. With their combination of plastic figures that draw in the home culture and other versatile objects, and the inviting immediacy of the medium, children can ride, cut across or completely recast all sorts of narrative codes.

Legitimizing diversity

Schools can work at enabling children to provide themselves with the cultural diet they need at different points in their lives. The teacher who cultivated 'interested mockery' was helping pupils to laugh at themselves and set off spicy dialogues which glamorized differences. My own work threw up opportunities to become aware of pressure and tolerance. Dredging up personal histories of toys, books and films established the existence of the multiple personalities that lived inside us. Supporting individual children who came into the open about unusual tastes offered a topsy-turvy background against which children with narrower tastes might consider adding a few extra items to their own cultural baggage. We practised holding back on being judgemental when people were opening up.

David: My favourite book is *Alice in Wonderland* 'cos they do strange things.
Peter: My favourite is fairy-tales.
[Darren laughs at Peter, I take him up on this.]
Darren: I like adventure stories [turns to Peter and delivers a coded apology] – don't laugh at me!

Our ongoing exchanges put these issues on the agenda as worthy concerns: children decided, for example, to interview children of the same age together so they didn't 'rubbish each other', and they considered audio tape as a possibly less intimidating interview medium than video. However, once metamorphosed into actual interviewers, carried away by the power of the camera, they committed major crimes of intimidation.

COMPETING WITH MURDOCH AND DISNEY

Comfortable schools

I have a fanciful vision of schools as bastions of diversity, dedicated to celebrating the paradoxical, the quirky and the minuscule. Teachers, with their slightly disreputable scatty values, would offer an anarchic playground, away from the earnest machinations of the gigantic culture machines, an alternative experience that would be interactive and warm (rather than pristine or politically correct), where children might come in and draw breath away from soulless game galleries that shudder away repetitively into the night, or from crushing special effects films, somewhere where children might be glad to be able to hear themselves think and then, hopefully, even be able to say something completely silly. We may not be able to compete with $200 million movies, but with shoe-string Monty Pythonesque voices we can play at David and Goliath, and feel powerful inside our small and valued kingdoms. One real-life moment captures this for me, to do with the power of tiny things: unseen to all but the rolling camcorder Kerry comes up to it, and briefly offers it a look through her pretend spectacles, a friendly gesture launched at unknown future audiences and popping out at me weeks later at home, on tape, like a jack-in-the-box that made my day.

Setting up meeting grounds

More sensible and easier to work towards is a vision of schools as meeting-places for our respective cultures. Neither party is claiming to know 'all about' the other side; both are making the effort to be open and to move onto territory that is likely to be accessible to the other. They are committed to finding meeting-points which will set up a proliferation of cultural cross-connections and breathe new life into their own personal reference systems, and into their relationship. The pupils are confident and perky because they feel they are contributing goodies that are worth something and will blow the socks off their old teacher and her cultural repositories. They also feel good because their knowledge and skill, like their great memory for visual detail, for example, is being honoured. Over time, anticipation, mutual respect and enjoyment grow. Because of the prime-time curriculum space this new approach receives, children find themselves getting better at perceiving and articulating complex meanings, and a ramified consciousness grows around aspects of their experience which had hitherto often just sloshed around at the back of their minds. The teacher too feels healed because suddenly the disused narratives that had had nowhere to go – the children didn't want to know – have been given fresh clothes and prime-time space, and her head is once more buzzing with cross-connections. Children reach out for more books, the teacher slips out to hire the latest video. Each savour their respective cultural products with a pleasure enhanced by further evocations and find old friends in new places. Let's sketch a tentative scenario.

The children usher in *The Mask*, the 1994 hit film about the repressed young man who puts on a mask (connected to Loki the God of Mischief), and transforms by night into a hedonistic and anarchic comic genius who can do anything he wants. Round 1 in the classroom, and the teacher tosses in narratives of people locked in spells by night and of metamorphoses; the children quickly throw in werewolves. On to the narratives of Jekyll and Hyde, Dorian Gray and a sprinkling of Freudian theory. Then to larger-than-life hedonists and anarchic heroes, Bottom, Gargantua, the Turtles. Enter the glittering Faust, and the Lords of Misrule, the Pied Piper, carnivals and show-offs, fools and jesters. Call up people who come into power, mad kings and sorcerers' apprentices. Enter mischief-makers, Puck, Reynard, Harpo Marx, Bugs Bunny. The teacher can haul in myriad trickster gods from every culture, Anansi, Raven, Hermes, Hanuman, and can read to the children the original Norse stories about Loki, referred to in the film. The children are excited about the Mask's plastic elasticity. The teacher throws in Alice, Anthony Browne and other surreal transformations. They can top up on classic animations from Tex Avery, whose elastic and intelligent humour inspires *The Mask*. There is endless delight in the Mask's virtual pockets, out of which come the most disruptive items. Refer back to Robin Williams' wisecracking showbiz genie in Disney's *Aladdin* and pull out Anthony Browne's Bear, who, with his ingenious pencil, can create any amount of disruption and save the day. Take a quick dash back to the fairy stories where girls on the run and witches on their heels toss magic combs over their shoulders. Talking of the mischievous objects in the Mask's pockets the children come back to Disney's *Beauty and the Beast,* with those little cups and teapots that have a life of their own. Cinderella, the Ugly Duckling, the Idiot and Orpheus come into it too, as do people who are tempted by power and renounce it: even the Gospels might get a star turn, and the distant figure of Jesus become invested with some of the lovability of Jim Carrey. For the sake of little people who quickly need to go back to elementary familiar icons, all can tramp back out and compare the Mask with other superpersons: the children might need to outdo themselves in communicating clearly with a teacher who doesn't know her Supermans from her Robocops. The teacher can mobilize curriculum time to enable the children to explore earnestly what larger-than-life deep self would emerge if *they* had a go at wearing the mask. (She recognizes with a grateful nod of acknowledgement in the direction of the children that this is indeed a more refreshing assignment than the make-three-wishes routine.) At this point, with a little skill, she might be able to encourage a little girl to wonder aloud why the mask gets to be worn by a male goody, a male baddy and a male dog, but why the girl in the film never gets a turn and only stays awkwardly tied to a post during most of the action. Children might embark on writing competing sequels to *The Mask,* and get into storyboarding, posters and trailers, in the delicious knowledge that the genuine article, a second *Mask* film, is actually coming into existence at this very point in time, somewhere across the Atlantic. Hopefully, there will also be plenty of cross-curricular time to work on how the film was made, and the skilful information-gatherers in the popular culture networks can keep their ears pricked.

Rival attractions on the audio-visual front

Just as we might open up ancient literary treasures to children, as long as we let them take us to the kinds of places where they feel comfortable enough to enjoy being with us, so too we sit on other neglected treasure hidden to them. There are a hundred years' worth of breathtaking and imaginative works from the cinema lying around which might speak very directly to children, because they are written in the language they know, for they are the children of an audio-visual age. They would feed strange and potent things into their imaginations. The children know nothing about them or have dismissed them because they're old. We are in a position to provide spaces where children can give themselves a chance to experience these potent 'texts'. A teacher at the school described how, after they had studied the Shakespeare play, the teachers gave children two film versions of *Julius Caesar* and let them choose which one they wanted to see first: the colour BBC version or the black and white version (with Marlon Brando). The children went for colour, of course, but later realized that the black and white film towered over the other, and they greatly savoured the moments of high drama, as when Marlon Brando appears carrying Caesar's body against a background of the mob.

Standard learning experiences can be tacked on to any committed exploration, so why not choose pleasurable and emotionally satisfying ones? Talking to me, Peter's mother compared children's interest in the media with the interest which children from an earlier and more rural age had for nature. She said that in those days schools capitalized on that interest and knowledge and did lots of nature studies precisely because children loved it and would work hard because of that. We seem to have forgotten that principle. We are living in the age of the streamlined and 'delivered' curriculum and struggle with shoe-string resources to engage the vast capabilities of children in a curriculum from which we have sidelined passion, playfulness and pleasure, while Murdoch and the big culture machines are being allowed to engage children's desires and command their trust and affection. There are some ways forward. We must first and foremost nourish our own inner child to make it strong and playful again, so it can guide us. To take up the desolate quote that closes Gill Venn's chapter at the end of this book we should at least aim to reclaim sufficient spaces for ourselves and our children for them to be able to say 'I really liked being 9.'

NOTES AND FURTHER READING

1 Stephen Kline, *Out of the Garden: Toys and Children's Culture in the Age of TV Marketing*, Verso, 1993, p. 277.
2 Bob Dixon, *Playing Them False: A Study of Children's Toys, Games and Puzzles*, Trentham Books, 1990.

3 Kline, op. cit.

4 The *Power Rangers* movie, for example, arranges for all the Rangers' old powers to fail and issues them with new ones. The set of animals giving power to each Ranger changes from prehistorical to modern, ushering into toy shops a whole new range of fighting machines to replace the Dinozords.

5 Cary Bazalgette, *Primary Media Education – a Curriculum Statement*, British Film Institute, 1989, p. 3.

6 Joseph Campbell, *The Hero with a Thousand Faces*, Paladin, 1949.

7 At the time of writing the latest major book of research reasserts the failure of the direct 'effects' model to establish a case for itself, despite enormous efforts. David Gauntlett, *Moving Experiences: Understanding Television's Influences and Effects*, Institute of Communications Studies, Leeds, 1995.

8 Kevin Durkin, *Television, Sex Roles and Children*, Open University Press, 1985, pp. 69, 68.

9 Bob Hodge and David Tripp, *Children and Television*, Polity Press, 1986.

10 D. Buckingham, *Children Talking Television: The Making of Television Literacy*, The Falmer Press, 1993.

11 Cary Bazalgette and David Buckingham (eds), *In Front of the Children: Screen Entertainment and Young Audiences*, British Film Institute, 1995, p. 7.

12 David Morley, *Family Television: Cultural Power and Domestic Leisure*, Comedia, 1986, p. 24.

13 Marina Warner, *Managing Monsters: Six Myths of Our Time – The Reith Lectures 1994*, Vintage, 1994.

14 See Maire Messenger Davis, *Television is Good for Your Kids*, Hilary Shipman, 1989, on the impact of the death of a soap character.

15 Cathy Pompe, 'When the Aliens Wanted Water' in Morag Styles (ed.), *After Alice: Exploring Children's Literature*, Cassell, 1992.

16 David Buckingham studies *The Big Breakfast* in his chapter in Cary Bazalgette and David Buckingham, op. cit.

17 Bazalgette, op. cit.

18 Annabelle Dixon, 'Storyboxes: Supporting the Case for Narrative in the Primary School', *Cambridge Journal of Education*, 17(3), 1987.

Part III

Ways of helping

In the final two chapters we consider some of the multifarious ways that older children read and use the products and messages of the popular culture industry. Our industrial society is now so complex that in crossing over into adulthood the developing child must learn an incredibly wide set of interpretative skills, face a variety of tests and multiple choices about how to be. At the same time, other things are happening: the childish body is beginning to change, the peer group resounds with new authority as parents begin to recede in day-to-day care and attention, and cultural messages which had previously been a source of pleasure and amusement, begin to have a new, shrill and worrying relevance. As children grow to 10, 11, 12 years of age, they have to make choices and decisions. Desire becomes sharpened and more sexually articulated. Yet, as we know, this is not, as it often seems for the participants, the end of change. All the same, this beginning of a fusion of sexual and social maturity can seem a stark and dramatic time, a time when teachers' sensitive behaviour can make an enormous difference, particularly with regard to understanding, using, rejecting or transforming cultural messages.

In Chapter 5 Gill Venn examines a group of young adolescent girls' perceptions of the images of femininity that they see in the various media and she considers the relationship of popular culture to the reality of their experiences. Through empirical work in an East London school that has a multi-ethnic intake, she explores issues to do with the girls' reading, both of their own choice and of the compulsory texts of the school curriculum. She shows through the girls' own comments the match and mismatch of school culture and popular culture to the different cultural backgrounds of the girls. Through samples of their writing, surveys of their magazine readings and direct references to the girls' expressed views, she also shows the great difference, already pointed out by other scholars, between the 11-year-olds' perceptions of themselves, active and questioning, and the 12- and 13-year-olds' more worrying acceptance of a diminished adult female role. She points to how teachers can help girls through this stage, particularly again through literacy practices which address the problems of their growing selves.

In Chapter 6 Isobel Urquhart explores images of masculinity that are deeply significant to a small but representative group of 11- and 12-year-old boys. She examines the warrior images and often violent narratives that these boys watch, use and reconstruct, both in writing and speech in school and in their peer groups. She considers in depth the meanings that the boys derive from aspects of popular culture which are often dismissed or deplored by teachers in school. She addresses questions to do with the kinds of masculinity represented in the boys' play and written texts, describing the uses fantasy of this sort has for the boys. She shows why reading literary fiction often falls away at this age and explores how boys position themselves towards school, popular culture, anger and violence and, in their fictional writing, towards the lost language of emotion.

Chapter 5

'I don't know where I am with myself'

The later years of childhood – constructions of femininity

Gill Venn

Literature? It's all about connecting lives.

(Anne, an English teacher, 1995)

September, and the new year 7 pupils arrive. Each year I'm amazed at the openness and direct manner of many of these 11-year-old girls. They often exude excitement about the world and their place within it and they will actively engage in discussions which require frank exchanges of opinions. This sense of purpose and self is also often expressed in their writing.

February in year 8, and the girls are now 12 or 13. During a personal, social and health education session, they are involved in activities designed to encourage discussion about potential future careers. The girls are now silent at the start of the lesson. When pushed to respond their replies seem guarded and unsure. The views expressed appear very limited, with resigned talk of marriage and babies. These girls, once quite self-assured and determined to find adventure and excitement in their lives, are now reticent about expressing their opinions. They seem to be limiting their own options, or even denying potential futures for themselves other than the 'traditional' view of motherhood and marriage.

I was fascinated and disturbed by this apparent shift and its impact on the girls' immediate involvement with work at school. What was happening? Was it the image of self as female that was altering, and how and why could such a shift take place so rapidly over a relatively short period of time? Was there a relationship between this shift and the girls' reading and writing? If we accept a model of literacy learning where texts challenge children's consciousness, then what was the relationship between the views these young girls had of themselves and the texts they were being exposed to? Young girls in the first two years of secondary school are confronted with a range of images of femininity from a variety of sources. How they are encouraged to accept or resist these images via their reading and writing was the central focus for my research and of this chapter.

Many arguments have been made concerning the potential clash of ideology between popular culture and high culture and the ensuing issues that arise relating to children's literacy and development. Many teachers are worried about the impact of popular culture on their pupils and about the difficulties of enabling children to access and to engage with 'deeper' literature which is embedded in high culture. Whilst recognizing this potential ideological disparity between popular and high culture, I would wish to add a third dimension, that of the home culture. With this addition, it would mean that in terms of images of femininity and self, young teenage girls are exposed to three potentially opposing strands: first, media representation of popular culture; second, high culture represented by the school; and third, home culture, which for children of different class or race from the dominant school culture may provide a very different view. Within this third strand there are interesting possible differences with regard to images of femininity. It is difficult to avoid stereotyping here, but it is perhaps useful to consider briefly some of the differing stereotypical images of women. Western media presentation of women, with the accompanying obsession of bodily perfection and fashion priorities, provides an interesting comparison with the traditional image of the Muslim woman who is private and covered. There are perhaps some links here with women in Western 'high' culture who are often presented as thoughtful, romantic and domesticated. Add to these an image of Afro-Caribbean women as being strong and matriarchal, and it is clear that girls from a variety of cultural backgrounds will be presented with a variety of images of women and femininity. I was interested in how, if at all, this variety of images impacted upon the girls' notions of self and their relationship with the world around them.

I conducted a small-scale study in an East London comprehensive which aimed to focus on the attitudes and perceptions of girls in years 7 and 8 (11–13 years old) and of their female English teachers. The girls were from a range of cultural backgrounds: white, Afro-Caribbean, Asian, Turkish, Italian and dual heritage. Most came from families that would describe themselves as working class. The teachers had all worked in the school for a significant number of years and had taught the girls since the beginning of year 7. The school prides itself on its commitment to equal opportunities, with staff and pupils working together on joint policies and action. The pupils and staff are therefore quite attuned to some of the more rehearsed notions of equality of opportunity. This chapter aims to expose the reader directly to the views and perceptions of both pupils and staff involved in the project.

Throughout the period of my study, there was one constant apparent difference between the 11/12- and the 12/13-year-old groups which directly reflected my original concerns. The 11-year-old girls were extremely open and seemed genuinely excited by the questions I was asking and by each other's answers. They had strong opinions on their favourite magazines, on the images of women being presented to them and, most importantly, of themselves. They seemed very clear both about their current positions and their futures. This was in stark contrast to the 12/13-year-old groups. Each answer to my questions was prefaced with hesitation and doubt. 'I don't know', 'I'm not sure' featured heavily in the taped interviews. Wishing to make some sense of this I looked to other authors and discovered that this 'shift' from the certain to the hesitant and uncertain has been documented by Mikel Brown and Gilligan in *Meeting at the Crossroads* (1992), their study of women's psychology and girls' development.

> Over the years of our study, even as they became more sophisticated cognitively and emotionally, young girls who had been outspoken and courageous in both an ordinary and a heroic sense became increasingly reluctant to say what they were feeling and thinking or to speak from their own experience about what they knew.
>
> (Mikel Brown and Gilligan, 1992: 217)

Such a shift needs to be recognized by schools and acted upon, particularly in the personal and creative domains such as personal, social and health education, art, drama and English. This process of dissociation at a time of significant physical development can be traumatic for girls. Being exposed to supportive texts or encouraged to explore their thoughts through their writing might be of real help. As one of the teachers involved in this study said:

> that's what literature is all about. It's about what's in you, what's out there and the writer sharing it with you and letting you unlock what's in you.

POPULAR CULTURE: MEDIA IMAGES OF FEMININITY AND GIRLS' REACTIONS TO THESE

All the girls were asked to list their favourite TV programmes and films and to give reasons for their choices. Having listened to pupils' conversations about their television viewing for a number of years, there were no real surprises in their choices which included soaps, both Australian and British, teen drama and comedy. Their comedy choices included programmes clearly aimed at black audiences and those aimed at white audiences – if it is possible to distinguish in this way. Their choices on the comedies did not reflect their ethnic background, that is, white pupils cited 'black' comedy such as *Fresh Prince of Bel Air* as a favourite. Only one pupil cited an adult drama programme as a favourite. Reasons for their choices included humour and the sense of programmes reflecting real life as they perceive it. They clearly liked programmes that explored teen 'angst', relationships and life crises, this being how they defined 'real life'. The fact that programmes were centred around the teen years was also important to them:

> It's mostly about teenagers and it's quite funny and interesting.

> They are young and fast. It's exciting and lots of suspense.

Soaps were also praised for the quality of acting and their structure:

I like it [*Eastenders*] because it ends at a good point and I have to watch it the next time.

Australian soaps were twice as popular as British-based ones. It is perhaps clear that they are more aimed at this age group, with story lines centred around the favoured teenage angst. Returning to their comedy preferences there were as many choices made for comedies centred around black families/young people as were made for those comedies which portrayed white youth and humour. Black, Asian and white pupils cited the black comedies as their favourites. There was a general sense that the majority of TV is not aimed at their age group and that they often feel 'in-between', i.e., not fitting the children's TV slot or the adult programmes. Although a number of adult programmes were watched, they did not feature in the 'favourite' selection. There was a general sense that *Eastenders* was of real interest to them as, although they did not feel that it related directly to their experiences, both Asian and black families appeared regularly in the story line, which was seen as a positive feature of this particular soap.

The categories of magazines read by both year groups were quite diverse. All the 11/12-year-old pupils cited teen magazines such as *Sugar* and *Just Seventeen* as at least one of their choices. Turkish and Indian magazines were also mentioned within this group by the Turkish and Asian girls. TV 'gossip-type' magazines were mentioned as being of real interest. With the older girls, the teen magazines cited were more limited, and a greater number of pupils claimed not to read magazines at all, as these were perceived as being completely alien to the home culture or religion:

I don't read them no more because I'm more into Islamic books.

This aversion to magazines is interesting in that it was not representative of a wholesale rejection of popular culture. The same pupil cited *Sweet Valley High* and *Sweet Valley Twins* as her favourite types of books, alongside 'Islamic books'. She also stated that her favourite TV programmes were Australian soaps and American comedies. Yet, in answer to the question, 'Who is your favourite group/singer and why do you like them?' she said:

None. Because I don't listen to a lot of music and singers do a lot of stupid things.

Teen magazines were clearly the overall favourite across both groups. Reasons for choosing to read these magazines were mainly centred around the fact that they reveal other people's lives, that they focus on teen-type interests and that they explore the whole arena of feelings and problems.

A breakdown in terms of content of the teen magazines cited bought in one week in February 1995 can be seen in the table below.

Type of article	Number of articles
Gossip	27
Relationships/romance	25
Fashion	14
Horoscopes	10
Problems	9
Readers' letters	7
Health & beauty	6
Entertainment	3
Fiction	3
Arts (your poems)	1
Current affairs	1

By far the most frequent articles were concerned with gossip and relationships. This would clearly equate with preferences stated regarding television viewing. Current affairs featured only once in one magazine.

The fiction content was one photo story, one written story and one novel, *The Boyfriend Club: Ginger's First Kiss*, which was provided free of charge with the *Just Seventeen* magazine (8 Feb. 1995). Other common elements were free giveaways and advertisements, which were naturally aimed at the age group.

I was deeply interested in the way in which the girls respond to the images of girls and women as portrayed by the magazines:

They encourage you to stay single 'cos of all the stories about people getting dumped and stuff.

I think magazines encourage you to go out with boys but not to get married.

One of the magazines reviewed during this week contained a sealed booklet on 'You and Your Body'. It was advertised on the front cover thus:

Free! body book. Intimate facts about you and him! (it's so hot it's sealed)

One of the 11-year-old girls said:

My brother ripped it out. He got angry and ripped it out 'cos he didn't want it to encourage me. He's 21. It tells you what's gonna happen to your body and he just ripped it out and put it in the bin. He thinks it's gonna encourage me to have sex ... It wasn't a nice feeling. I felt as if he was thinking that I was gonna have sex and it wasn't a nice feeling.

The fact that nearly all the models used by the magazines were white was also noted by the girls. In the magazines cited by the girls, there were no Asian models and only one black model featured. One Asian pupil tried to explain:

In our religion, you shouldn't sing or dance or stuff so we shouldn't be in magazines.

This statement provoked a heated discussion amongst the Islamic pupils as to the varying requirements of their faith being dependent upon the mosque attended. With reference to the lack of different races portrayed, one pupil commented:

It's racist. All the girls are white and blonde and they all look the same.

I got this week's *Sugar* and there were loads of hairstyles. There were one or two black people and all the rest were white.

Clearly, for many girls, their home cultures are not being

reflected in the popular culture. Discussing self-image, ideal self and potential discrepancies between the two, Denis Lawrence (1988) explores the notion that building on the foundations laid by parents and early schooling, the older child begins to compare him/herself with peers, particularly in terms of body image. Lawrence states:

> Peer comparisons are particularly powerful at adolescence. The influence of the media also becomes a significant factor at this time with various advertising and show business personalities providing models of aspiration.
>
> (Lawrence, 1988: 4)

The implications of this are clear. The potential for these pupils' self-esteem to be affected by this continual absence of images reflecting their home culture should perhaps be addressed by teachers and schools. Schools alone cannot combat the mainstream Eurocentric images purveyed by the mass media, but the opportunity for providing a balance needs to be explored. This is where literature, discussion and a model of literacy that works with individual consciousness could be deeply effective. It is therefore important to explore the role of 'high' culture within the school.

THE SCHOOL AS HIGH CULTURE

The potential for each girl crossing over between popular texts and high literature could come within the area of pupils' choice of books for reading themselves. However, by far the most popular choice for pupils in both year groups was the Point series, including *Point Horror* and *Point Romance* books. Judi Blume was also cited as a favourite, as was Roald Dahl. When I asked the girls about the images of women as portrayed in the books they read, some of the responses were quite startling, as can be seen by the following comments, which came from both age groups:

— They're the ones who get upset, killed or dumped.

— Dumped, raped, depressed, murdered, fall in love, mugged . . .

— Something bad always happens to them.

— Depressed, something bad or falls in love, raped, sexually abused . . .

— In 'Sweet Valley' most of them are heroes, but in other books men dominate.

— They always end up crying or rowing.

— They help their friends and sometimes save the day. Usually they're minor characters.

— In stories they say that they are beautiful and have a good voice and things like that.

I feel that such images could surely be balanced by more positive images provided by texts read at school. However, the girls' perception of school-based books was not entirely positive. Most felt that the school library should contain more books of the *Point Horror* genre and that books studied in class were often of more interest to the boys. This perception could be due to a range of factors, including the possibility that teachers are taking the girls' literacy for granted and trying to gain the interest of the boys. The following is taken from a group conversation about books read in school:

— They're silly books. Even the love books, they don't tell you anything.

— Judi Blume is brilliant. There's this book and all these teenagers write in and tell her stuff about menstruation, masturbation and she's good.

— *Would you ever read Judi Blume with your teacher?*

— No never! She'd never let us because she likes books like *The Silver Sword* and stuff about the olden days.

— She'd be embarrassed to talk about it.

— It could be difficult as there's boys around.

— It's just war stuff and you can't get into it.

— No. I think it's interesting.

So their opinions about the content of many school texts were often negative. The teachers too clearly feel constrained to a point by the type of texts they feel they can present to pupils.

When discussing the girls' alienation from the texts, one teacher said,

> the National Curriculum has done that. It's so structured. The hidden agenda of the National Curriculum is to play up the academic and to play down the pastoral role totally. It's dying ... by overloading people with work and creating a formal structure.

Even if the choices for the teacher were completely open, there might still be a divide between the popular culture choice of the pupils and the higher culture choice of the school. Many teachers choose to work with and from the pupils' original choices, aiming to lead them into exploring more open choices. Examples were cited by the teachers of pupils showing an interest in a theme, of suggesting a book to the pupil and of the pupil returning later with enthusiasm and joy at having read the recommended text.

However, books are not the only means of a school presenting its culture and value systems. Assemblies are a useful measure of what is valued by the school. The school featured in this study has a carefully thought through assembly policy and it is clearly the intention that all cultures and both genders should be represented and valued openly via the assemblies. But again, the pupils' responses were far from positive:

— They're just long lectures about how the school should be treated.

— Yeah, massive lectures about how the school gets vandalized.

— They think the school is more important than anything in the world.

If the assemblies weren't actively endorsing positive roles and values, I was interested in the position of women teachers as role models.

> All they [women teachers] show us is work and go home, work and go home, nothing else, just work and go home. They don't show anything about their personal life or being a woman or anything.

They don't tell you nothing. All school is for me is about science, geography, maths, that sort of stuff.

Both these comments were made by 11-year-old girls. The older girls were divided in their opinions, which seemed to reflect differences in their relationships with their form tutors. Where the form tutor was young and female, there was a real sense that teachers do have an impact, that they are very approachable and are prepared to discuss issues with pupils. The second older group have had a succession of form tutors due to organizational difficulties and these girls shared the sense of alienation from female staff as do the younger girls who are still relatively new to the school. This has clear implications for continuity in the secondary school, either via the form tutor system or via subject teachers. One 11-year-old girl said:

I think primary school teachers are much better. At my last school I could talk to any female teacher.

Another added:

In my last school I had this teacher, Ms P., and you could talk to her about anything. I still go and see her now.

A third girl joined in the conversation with:

In primary you've got more time with a teacher. You spend the whole year with her.

This dilemma for women teachers is highlighted by Mikel Brown and Gilligan (1992) in their discussion of the role models available to adolescent girl pupils:

One of the most difficult questions for women teachers was whether it was legitimate for them to show girls their sadness and their anger, and also whether they could reveal such feelings without losing control of themselves and of the girls. It seemed easier and also safer for women to try and model perfection for girls.

THE HOME CULTURE

There was a real sense amongst all the year 7 girls that the expectation from home was that they were to be 'good':

My parents want me to be a good little girl, sit at home and do my homework.

Like when the bell goes – just go home. Don't ask to go anywhere, just go home, get changed, do the housework, sit down, do your homework, that's it.

However, it was these same younger girls who gave their responses immediately when asked about how they would see themselves in ten years' time. They all shouted – with enthusiasm:

— I'll be in America.

— I'll be travelling.

Three girls said, at the same time,

— I'll be free!

This was in direct contrast to the older girls who, when asked the same question, all hesitated. There was a long silence before anyone spoke up. Each response was prefaced with 'I don't know' or 'I'm not sure'. One 13-year-old pupil said after a pause:

I used to want to be a doctor. Now I think I want to be a hairdresser.

This uncertainty may well stem from the process of dis-sociation as described by Mikel Brown and Gilligan (1992). It might also link with a growing awareness of personal strengths and perceived weaknesses – as compared to the rest of the class, for example (cf. Lawrence, 1988). Such lack of certainty could and should be used by the school. Writing activities which encourage the girls to explore their confusions have been very successful. The following passage is from a 13-year-old girl's writing that was prompted by an RE lesson on journeys of life:

My journey has been a sad one, a happy one, a peaceful one and a painful one. This journey is the journey of my life. From my birth till my death I will be on this journey and perhaps there will be another journey after this.

This journey I am writing about is not a physical journey, it is about my feelings, my hopes and my fears. In this journey I have experienced many things. I have travelled far and wide and have come back with nothing except knowledge. I continue to learn. I am a dreamer and in my dreams is the hope that as I go through this journey I will learn from my mistakes. There was one thing I always wanted to know and that is why am I here, why was I born, what is the point of life?

At this point in my life I am confused, I don't know where I am with myself, I don't know where I'm going. I think it is unfair to me because I had no choice to ask if I was to make this journey or not and I have no choice to when this journey ends. In this journey I will try to be happy.

There are clear implications for the writing context and environment which need to be 'safe' and which provide an atmosphere of trust for such highly autobiographically voiced writing. This, in turn, has implications for the relationship between pupil and teacher. The RE teacher was working with a group of 13-year-old pupils about loss. One pupil whose mother had committed suicide two years earlier started to write about her. This boy had previously refused to communicate on any level about the mother's death, including rejecting bereavement counselling. When asked later why he had chosen this lesson to start to write about his mother, he replied:

I feel safe with Ms X. When I started to cry about it she let me sit in her office with N (his friend) . . . later she came and talked about it all.

This child clearly felt 'safe' with Ms X. It could be argued that her skills and warmth enabled him to start to explore his feelings about his huge loss. The texts that the class had been using to introduce the pupils to the notion of 'loss', combined with the established relationship between pupil and teacher, had triggered the exploration through writing.

To return to the potential home influence on life choices, I asked the girls about parental attitudes to possibilities for the future. The expectations of marriage showed differences across the age and ethnic groups. The Asian girls all held the perception that the expectation was that they would marry, eventually, usually after further study and possibly a career:

My parents want me to get married when I'm older, but I'm not sure.

My mum wants me to go to college and get a degree and live. But my dad just wants me to study and be brainy.

The pupil who had earlier rejected elements of the popular culture was tentative about marriage but had a strong sense of her future:

I think I'll get married in the future. I want to be a strong Muslim and a famous Muslim.

With the older girls there was once again the sense of uncertainty:

They'd like me to go to college when I leave school. I don't really wanna go but I'm not sure.

These older pupils were also keen to discuss the possibility of having children:

My mum don't want me to have children until I'm older and so I can have a career first, but I'll probably have 'em when I'm 15 to get it over and done with.

I wanna have twins, but I don't wanna get married.

As seen earlier, I found that the influence of male figures at home is significant for the girls. The sense of overprotection is keenly felt by the girls, who seem to find it difficult to cope with the restrictions and even advice when it is offered. When discussing who they would turn to with problems or questions about sex, one year 7 pupil said:

My dad, he talks to me about things like that and I get really embarrassed.

Their views of marriage generally seem to be affected both by the images portrayed in the popular culture and their direct experiences of home. The following is an extract from a conversation between the younger girls about marriage:

— It's like, if you're married right, you have a commitment – like for all my life right. I wanna live my life for me, do whatever you want, 'cos when you're married, you got certain responsibilities. There's things you can't do that you can do when you're single.

— If you're married to someone you can't go out and see

other people because then you'll be feeling sorry for who-
ever you're married to. And like sometimes, usually
when you get married, things slow down and you end
up staying at home and not doing much.

— Well I don't wanna get married 'cos I wanna get to do
things, the things that people do ... I just wanna get
older and get on with it. If I got married it would be like
now but even worse.

— When you get married, your problems start. A husband's
even worse than a mother you know ... Trouble starts
when you get married, it's best to stay single.

Encouraging the girls to explore these images of femininity
and of their potential futures that they receive from the home
culture is vital and could possibly be achieved through writing
creatively and exploring the issues in groups. In this way, the
girls can use texts to enrich and develop their growing subjectivities.

CULTURAL DISSONANCE

If it is accepted that there is potential dissonance between the
three major cultural influences on pupils – the popular, home
and 'high' literature – the school needs to address this and create
a potential arena for pupil exploration of the issues involved. I
would argue that personal and social education sessions would
be one forum for discussion of such issues, but that English has
a substantial role to play in this disentanglement of imagery
and messages for pupils.

Before the introduction of the National Curriculum, many
teachers of English saw their contact time as an opportunity for
such exploration by the pupils. Writing in 1977, Michael Yorke
discussed the findings of his survey into the attitudes of English
teachers to the subject. He found that teachers were following
in the Leavisite tradition and that they perceived literature as:

fostering understanding, toleration, moral standards, love of
the beautiful, and as offering insight into the relationship
between human kind and nature. They saw it as relaxing, and
yet cathartic ... Literature for older pupils should include

themes such as death and loss, the understanding of self and society, and should involve considerations of moral concern.

(Sarland, 1991)

Unfortunately, there is not space here to discuss the impact of the National Curriculum on the nature and value of English, but if it is to continue to provide opportunities for pupils actively to engage with and explore attitudes and images, appropriate texts and methodology should be employed. As one teacher in this study said:

There is a view that English is a subject, a body of knowledge. My view is different. I see it as a way into children. Somehow you make them understand that they are ... That's what literature is and was about. Dickens didn't write what he wrote to get into a hall of fame, to become part of high culture – he wrote what he wrote because he wanted to say something about the world he lived in, and he wanted to create art and relate to people.

Sometimes the teaching of Shakespeare's works to younger pupils is cited as an example of cultural imperialism. As one of the teachers explained,

Shakespeare is seen as some sort of cultural passport, a rite of passage. If you know when the Battle of Trafalgar was and can name three Shakespeare plays, then you must be British.

So there is an understandable fear that working with Shakespeare with pupils from ethnic minorities could be seen as simply promoting the mainstream culture. However, the response from many parents from the minority communities is far from resistant. For many who undertook their education in the 'colonies', Shakespeare was a fundamental part of the curriculum and is regarded as something that is not only culturally acceptable but also as something that was extremely enjoyable. There is also a strong sense of ownership of the major writers due the English language link. They are therefore very supportive of the idea of their own children being exposed to such texts. The school in this study had very successfully used the BBC's *Shakespeare for the People* with the pupils, where the texts are brought to life and made immediately relevant to the pupils' experiences. One teacher told of the lesson where the pupils became very excited by the programme and were very keen to study more texts as a result.

Purves undertook a major international survey in 1973. In all the countries surveyed, it was suggested that the literature taught was drawn from the elite culture (Sarland, 1991). It would be interesting to study the cultural roots of the texts now employed by teachers following the National Curriculum. The inclusion of 'multicultural' texts is laudable and, indeed, vital if pupils' home cultures are to be genuinely valued. However, Whitehead, writing in 1988 sounded a useful note of caution:

> When people talk about multicultural fiction, they often mean no more than books which reflect our current multi-racial society by the inclusion of one or more characters from ethnic minorities. Motivation for such inclusion may be a response to the felt need of black Britons to be accepted as a natural and normal part of British society.
>
> (Whitehead, 1988: 4)

Texts which originate from these different cultures and which are a genuine reflection of the minority culture are therefore important to include within the syllabus. They can also be an exciting springboard for discussions of gender, with differing emphases often being highlighted.

THE IMPACT OF IMAGES AND CULTURAL INFLUENCES ON READING AND WRITING

Gemma Moss in *Unpopular Fictions* (1989) discusses the concept of popular culture being 'primarily the culture of consumption rather than production'. What is significant for the pupils of this study is how their relationship with images presented by this popular culture develops and is actively challenged by the pupils themselves. The younger pupils showed a clear under-standing of the manipulation of the magazines and popular fiction. They were clear about the stereotypical images being presented to them and were equally adamant that they challenge such images in their own writing:

> I'd include Asian women because there aren't any in books and magazines, but I'd write about them.

Most books talk about white people always. But I'd change that and have all sorts of people in my stories.

Unfortunately, the reality is that they tend to produce formulaic writing with white stereotypical characters, when they are writing creatively. The teacher's response is to aim continually to push the pupils into more analytical frameworks, to develop strategies for producing work which challenges the images and the popular formulae.

Challenging the images seems more likely to occur in the younger pupils when they are encouraged to write from a personal viewpoint. The following extract was presented to me by a year 7 pupil when we were part way through my study. It was a piece that she had written in year 6, immediately prior to leaving primary school.

When I grow up I am going to teach the boys who's boss. So when I grow up I'm going to go out a lot and have fun. When I grow up I'm going to play snooker and after that I'll go and ride my horse and let all my cats out and walk the dogs. Then once I have done them all I'll go for a super fast ride on my Fireblade (motorbike). Then I'll come home, let my cats back in, walk the dogs, and feed all the animals, and the hamsters and rabbits. Then I'll clear up and have dinner. Then I'll go to bed.

It was the older girls who showed a preference for writing love stories with the heroines re-enacting stereotypical responses in familiar contexts. Mikel Brown and Gilligan (1992) discussed this need for pupils to be encouraged to resist such images from the popular culture:

Moving into a culture populated by images and models of young women, girls incorporate these images from reading magazines and books, from watching TV and from listening-in on the ways that other people, especially parents and teachers, look at and speak about them, their classmates, their acquaintances, and friends. And girls need to hold themselves away from the power of images and voices which encourage them to label their feelings and desires and needs as 'selfish', and to see selflessness or self silencing as the condition for being loved or approved of.

(Mikel Brown and Gilligan, 1992: 175)

Thus, how teachers deal with gender issues in the classroom is of paramount importance to the children's growing consciousness. Ideological discussions at secondary level can be useful in personal and social education sessions, but it is the *immediate impact of literature* which can be of real use in bringing alive the issues for pupils. But one teacher issued a warning about the choice of texts:

> The material we've chosen to deal with gender is dry ... because it is a stereotype-breaking story about a princess and a knight. What it does is it removes the whole thing from a contemporary setting and any relevance to their lives. And so what you are looking at is how the writer does this, which is much more about English at its academic level – but what it's always been about for me is ways into the kids' own experiences – connecting.

Inspired and personal teaching can help pupils make those vital connections.

CONCLUSIONS

Thus, it seems vital that, as teachers, we aim to empower girls from all cultures to resist stereotypical images of femininity as portrayed by popular culture. English lessons in secondary school are ideal opportunities for encouraging pupils to understand the images that they are confronted with, to engage with such issues whilst reading for enjoyment and writing creatively. Bringing popular culture into the classroom as a medium for analysing and developing the pupils' skills of literary criticism can be constructive and can lead pupils into a wider range of texts and experiences. Discussing the potential inclusion of *Point Horror* texts into the classroom, one teacher stated:

> My personal response to having 'Point Horror' in the classroom is that if they're reading, then fine ... But if they are *only* reading *Point Horror*, then I am a little bit concerned because I like to lead them on to other things.

The same argument can apply to popular TV programmes and magazines. In discussing the magazines, all groups of pupils showed clear understanding of what was being presented and a degree of analysis of the mainstream images apparent through-out. The same sensitive teacher argued:

> One of the things we are about is providing an analytical faculty for them. And if they can use that, and apply it, and justify their choices, then I think – good for you, go for it. I don't think anyone's got the right to state that *Eastenders* isn't as good as something else. Whatever you think, with the benefit of an education, middle age, and the rest of it, it's not relevant really. As long as they are making informed choices, and not just being fed a diet of what somebody else tells them is right.

So it is evident that teachers who are developing literacy sensitively need to value the pupils as individuals, their cultures, their current interests and to be 'up front' about presenting choices and alternatives. Developing their literacy skills can be intrinsically linked with widening their choices, their horizons and their sense of personal possibilities. If, by studying appropriate texts and being afforded the opportunity to engage in real discussion of the issues involved, the pupils are more able to make informed decisions and choices, then the role of English in the secondary school is to be valued and cherished. As teachers we need to encourage and enable the older girls to rediscover their own voices through personal exploration and interaction with established texts.

> We heard this shift as a change in girls' voices as they reached adolescence. In essence, we were witnessing girls enacting and narrating dissociation. Women's psychological development within patriarchal societies and male voiced cultures, is inherently traumatic.
>
> (Mikel Brown and Gilligan, 1992: 216)

When asked if she liked being herself at this point, one 13-year-old pupil replied:

> I really liked being 5. I was happy then – at least my mum says I was.

Perhaps we can help her find her lost voice through sensitive classroom practice and by using a model of literacy which challenges and enriches her personal self. All the texts that she has to integrate from different sources during this time of change and her own transformation into womanhood can be developed through warmth and a wide acceptance and interrogation of a multiplicity of texts. This empowerment through literary exploration and critical understanding of the differing cultural influences needs to take place and be encouraged in the classroom. Perhaps then the lost voice will be found.

BIBLIOGRAPHY AND FURTHER READING

Brown, S. and Riddell, S. (eds) (1992) *Class, Race and Gender in Schools*, Glasgow: Scottish Council for Edinburgh Research in Education.

De Lyon, H. and Widdowson, M. (1989) *Women Teachers: Issues and Experiences*, Milton Keynes: Open University Press.

Gilligan, C. (1993) *In a Different Voice*, Boston, Mass.: Harvard University Press.

HMI (report) (1992) *The Preparation of Girls for Adult and Working Life*, London: Department of Education.

Lawrence, Denis (1988) *Enhancing Self-Esteem in the Classroom*, London: Paul Chapman Publishing.

Mikel Brown, L. and Gilligan, C. (1992) *Meeting at the Crossroads: Women's Psychology and Girls' Development*, Boston, Mass.: Harvard University Press.

Moss, Gemma (1989) *Unpopular Fictions*, London: Virago.

Sarland, C. (1991) *Young People Reading: Culture and Response*, Milton Keynes: Open University Press.

Verma, G. and Bagley, C. (eds) (1982) *Self-concept, Achievement and Multicultural Education*, London: Macmillan.

Whitehead, W. (1988) *Different Faces: Growing Up with Books in a Multicultural Society*, London: Pluto Press.

Chapter 6

'You see all blood come out'
Popular culture and how boys become men

*Isobel Urquhart**

Liam sits in the middle of the sofa, in his Manchester United football shirt, next to Dean in a similar top, who is leaning against his Mum. Liam says, with a look of shared understanding at Dean, 'Lots of girls like . . . *My Little Pony!*' They make derisive noises at each other, enjoying the fun. 'They make them *jump* and *fly*. "Ooh, I'm a *Little Pony!* Ooh, I'm *flying!*" ' They make mocking 'girlie' noises, squeals. They wave their arms about in the air, flapping their hands, laying their hands against their cheeks and raising their eyes to heaven in a parody-gesture of girlish excitement. 'Vapours' is the word that springs to my mind as the most apt description of their action. I interrupt, asking, 'How is that different from when you're playing with . . . *Box Master*, or the computer games? They jump and fly, don't they?' and Dean answers me, reflectively, 'Because most of ours have machine-guns.' He follows this explanation with machine-gun noises, accompanied by the common gesture of a two-fisted grip held centrally at about waist height, the hands made to vibrate in simulation of the kick of the machine gun. Then, as elaboration of this point, he excitedly tells me about Liam's computer game. 'On his game when we were playing it – there's this man walking round with a great big axe and when he throws it like that [Dean mimes the overarm throwing of an axe], all these little axes come up and he goes "Pmfff!" and [his voice thickens into a thrilled tone] you see all blood come out.'

INTRODUCTION

How do boys become men? I talked to a number of boys aged between 10 and 13 about the books, television, video films and computer games they enjoyed. In this chapter, all references to particular popular fictions were first referred to by the boys in the project. Jedd, 12 years old, and Terry, 11, were pupils who dictated stories to me, and Robbie and Barry, both aged 11, were selected by their head of year to advise me about computer games and videos I did not know. They were all pupils at the local comprehensive school where I used to teach. Dean and Liam, 10, live in the same street as me in the same new town near London. Andy, Tony and Kieron came from another school and were aged 11 and 12. Most could be described as growing up within working-class communities. In this chapter, I have tried to consider what meanings these 10- to 12-year-old boys were constructing from the content of the texts they read and watched, and from the activity of reading. Children's reading is defined, here, in a wide sense to include activities such as watching TV and films and playing with computer games and little media-related plastic toys of various types. The common factor for me was the children's willing entry into a fantasy world based on some form of mass-produced fiction.

What did the endless re-enactments of warriordom via TV animations, computer games, comics, videos, films, toys and games mean for them? Why did these fictions grip these boys so powerfully? Why did Terry, for example, dictate a three-chapter story, borrowing heavily from videos he had watched, in which he fled across continents from a man-monster intent on destroying him, whose repetitive murderous deeds he described with blood-curdling relish? Should I have praised his mastery of the genre or told him to imagine something more 'suitable'? Should I, as responsible teacher, demolish through my 'superior' critique these crazes that seem always to glorify violence and which demean the powerless, including women and other victims? A teacher told me of his dismay as he tried to dissuade a pupil from an apparently obsessive identification with a warrior-hero he admired on TV. The child, he reported, wept as one bereaved.

Teachers, and society in general, have been worrying about the effects of popular culture on children for a long time. When

I was young, there were heated debates about war comics and their part in the moral degeneration of 'Teddy Boys'. Recently, the same concerns have been expressed about *Teenage Mutant Ninja Turtles* and *Power Rangers*, for example. While our society produces and clearly enjoys – to judge from sales and audience ratings – popular culture, we are also disturbed by our fears about what children will learn from the fantasies we generate. In recent years, one major concern has been what children learn about their gender identity from the fantasies they are absorbed by. When the discussion turns to boys it takes the form of suggesting that boys watch and play warrior-hero fantasies, copy the behaviour of stereotypical characters and internalize masculine values embedded in the plot. They are then assumed to apply these cultural fantasies to their real-life behaviour. Evidence is produced, for example, in the form of children hurting each other in the playground by acting out flying kicks they have seen their warrior-heroes employ and, in its more alarmist form, by references to murders by children that are inferred to have been copies of horror films they were believed to have been watching. Less dramatically, teachers are concerned that children believe that the fantasies embody values that regulate real, adult life and will therefore aspire to those values, for instance, in gender-specific ways that perpetuate a society which does indeed treat people unequally according to their class, gender, race, ethnicity and religion.

I found myself asking whether the boys I taught learned masculine identities partly through popular fiction – identities that would lead them to resort to aggression and violence in their current lives as well as in their future adult lives, and that would shut them off from other solutions to conflict and from other, more emotional, more articulate ways, of relating to other people. Was there an argument for allowing these popular fictions a place in school? Were there implications for me, a woman teaching young boys? How did my own gender influence what I valued or deplored in their writing and the popular fictions they enjoyed? It seemed to me that popular culture alone and in itself could not be held responsible for such large, societal effects. However, what popular culture does perpetuate are narratives that we tell ourselves about deep-seated wishes and fears about ourselves and our relation to the world and other people. These narrative resolutions to unresolved anxieties come in gender-specific form, but the underlying anxieties are the same for all, in that they deal with our identity, its vulnerability, and the desire for safety and a sense of a predictable world. Nevertheless, the developmental process of forming an adult masculine identity means that boys read gender-specific solutions to these anxieties which they can use at a particular stage of their development to explore what it may mean to become a man. Thus, children make active choices and selections in how they use the offer of masculine identities as portrayed in popular culture. It may be, however, that for some boys, where other circumstances confirm their powerlessness and lack of achievement in school and society, fantasies of total physical supremacy and triumph of will might, 'in effigy' as Freud calls it, meet very profound experiences of desire and lack. This chapter is my exploration of some of these questions, through the popular fictions some boys talked about and my reflections, based on their conversations and stories, in which I have tried to learn something of the significance those fictions seemed to have for them.

However, just as women rightly claimed that they were better positioned to describe what women's experience meant to them, there remains for me some doubt about my own activity in reflecting upon masculine identity. My own identity as a teacher, of course, reflects a conformity to a feminine role as helper, and my experience has largely been in 'helping' unhappy and/or aggressive adolescent boys. My personal investment in understanding these young men, I now suspect, has something to do with the need subordinates have to know about those who dominate them. Women, it is argued, spend a lot of time understanding men, in order to protect their own well-being from the unpredictable effects of male power. We may speculate that women teachers may understandably wish to intervene in the development of masculine identities that have dominated and oppressed them.

Of course, we are not defined by our gender roles alone – other factors such as our social class, age, ethnicity and racial background also interconnect with gender to influence our identities in subtle and complex ways. Children's class, gender and ethnicity also affect how particular fictions and how the very activity of reading is perceived.[1] Children from different social communities have different expectations of what stories are, and are for, while schools seem often to reject the kinds of reading characteristic of some communities. It is important, therefore, not to think of boys as if they are essentially all the same. Individuals differ between and within particular cultural communities. Nevertheless, some similarities in experience lead to similarities in response, and it is at this modest level of generalization that I wish to discuss the social and cultural aspects of reading popular fiction among boys.

But I have also been conscious that boys *and* girls find in the particular gender-specific forms of romance or adventure narratives something powerfully pleasurable which seems to go beyond the functionally informative material about social gender roles. There are other ways of thinking about the value and purpose of reading for children that focus on the imaginative power that stories have and the significance of fantasy and desire in the activity of reading.[2] There is often something obsessive about the way children engage with fantasy. It was the repetitive, compulsive quality to the boys' interest in these popular fictions – markedly different from the slumped lethargy pupils would sometimes display when we 'did' reading in school – that intrigued me (why did they not get tired of the same old story?) and I have tried to explore the nature of that narrative desire. I believe that one way in which we can link how children learn about gender through reading, and what the emotional appeal of the warrior-story is for boys, might be to link the discussion about the development of gender identity to the boys' deep personal desire to know who they are and what they are in the world to be, i.e., the formation of an individual identity, which inevitably leads them to learn and try out the multiple social representations of masculinity.

The second section of the chapter considers the way talking about popular culture to friends seemed to emphasize the social representation of masculinity. Although the act of reading can be a solitary activity, the boys often used popular culture in their interactions with each other. They role-played scenes from films, they exchanged computer games and evaluated their interest-level, they watched TV together or later shared their reactions to TV and video programmes, and they played together with their Box Master toys or compared their collections of mini-Boglins. Boys began to tell other boys about being a man, and to play out and act out and talk out the representations of masculinity they had taken from the narratives they read and watched. In that process, a public discourse that amplified social idealizations of manhood seemed to be being developed and confirmed. Was something of the individual reader's complexity of response being left out?

Finally, in the third section, I considered what place school should have in relation to the working-class children I spoke to and their deep pleasures in their popular culture. Some of those images and narratives, it has long been argued, contribute to a perpetuation of social, economic and political inequalities between the sexes, because children learn to identify with and to comply, even against their own personal interests, with how society defines their role. As a teacher, therefore, I learned to examine the stories I offered children in school for stereotyped gender characteristics (e.g., Peter climbs the tree and Jane admires him) because I too believed that reading fiction teaches children about the world. I, too, wanted to ensure that, by offering fictions that disconfirmed dominant preconceptions about masculinity and femininity, children did not accept uncritically the sexual stereotypes that are present in our society and that they did learn other and wider repertoires of gender values and behaviours. Some of the roles, attitudes and behaviours that were conveyed as appropriate for girls or for boys in the films and books they like to read should, it seemed for me, then, be challenged and resisted because they confirmed an adult society in which, for example, women are still unable to claim equal working rights with men and in which women's experiences and needs have less significance and power, in the public arena, than men's. I also saw a world, *said* to be constructed to suit men's experiences and desires, that could in fact be a violent and dangerous place, particularly for young men themselves. Young men suffer more physical attacks than other sectors of the population, largely from other young men. The men who fight wars all over the world are mostly very young, barely out of their teens. But, as I watched the boys resist the school's blandishments for them to consider alternative gender models, what really set the boys alight were the fantasies of fast, often funny, but always powerful masculine aggression by strong, taciturn heroes who policed the world, meting out justice to evil-doers as a rationale for making their violence legitimate.

How could we, then, as teachers, properly respect and understand the pleasure and learning children gained from popular culture, and bring it into learning, without our smiling approval killing off its (often) subversive attractions or our moralizing disapproval putting yet more distance between the school's activities and our pupils' experiences. Yet the aims and instrumentality of a national curriculum in English say little that would encourage teachers to have confidence that prizing children's reading and narrative experiences out of school is part of the content we are exhorted to 'deliver'. And if we did, would the dead hand of education spoil its out-of-school pleasure? Popular culture for the working-class children I spoke to was popular partly because it *wasn't* about school, it *did* contradict school values, and it wasn't *work*. Like Willis's lads twenty years ago,[3] the boys I met were beginning to see their own identity and values as bound up with the inversion of whatever the school approved of. How do we avoid perpetuating attitudes that fail to find value, particularly in working-class boys' experiences outside school in ways which continue to disadvantage them in school?

SECTION 1: READING AND THE INDIVIDUAL READER

The inside story on the adult world

There is no doubt that pre-adolescent children read and use popular culture in order to know about the world. It is a 'prime tool . . . for gathering and organising information about the wider world and learning how that world works.'[4] Part of the way our society works is that we think of individuals as placed in a particular gender relation to other individuals. This generally obliges us to behave, talk and think of ourselves and others in ways that create and then demonstrate our identity as either boy or girl, man or woman. Children learn how society represents gender, and how to represent themselves as gendered, from a wide range of images, behaviour, and discourses in their environment, including representations in popular fictional narratives. For a certain period in their development, boys appear to be particularly interested in stories about male heroes involved in exciting adventures. Older adolescent boys and younger primary school-aged boys do not show the same marked preference. This suggests that it is at this time that boys become particularly interested in questions of adult masculine identity as it relates to their own developmental concerns.

As we know, masculine and feminine genders are stereotypically differentiated in terms of the power relations between them, in which masculinity is characterized by power, authority, aggression and technical competence, while femininity, associated with sociability, sexual passivity and acceptance of domesticity and motherhood, is seen as compliant with subordination to and accommodation of the interests and desires of men.[5] Much research has attempted to investigate how girls have learned to accept and comply with a subordinate identity to which mass culture and popular fictions, which rarely challenge stereotypical gender representations, appear significantly to contribute. Later research, however, demonstrates that girls and women do, in fact, resist compliance with the social roles ascribed to their sex in romance fiction and that they use romance fiction for purposes of their own, not simply to have 'caught' the genre and be under its influence.[6] Attention has, however, recently begun to turn to how boys are also subject to powerful pressures to comply with *oppressive* masculine roles, and that non-conformity for boys can sometimes be more problematic than it is for girls.[7] For example, Liam and Dean could think of girls who watched and enjoyed the same TV as they did and who played the same video games, but they could not think at first of any boys at all who didn't like gruesome things, such as 'all blood coming out'. Eventually, they did think of one, who was then described in terms which suggested that his *masculinity was automatically in question*: the same high-pitched voice used for mocking the girls was employed to describe his distress at the sight of blood.

Previously acquired gender characteristics influence the way girls and boys respond to texts. That is, they read texts differently, as well as reading different texts. For example, some boys and girls, aged 11 and 12, talking about literature they had read, talked in different ways about the book they were reading and, in doing so, could be described as simultaneously 'doing' gender.[8] The girls' talk about the book centred on feelings, relationships and caring. They were interested in plot details in so far as they shed light upon the development and deepening understanding of the characters. The boys' talk, on the other hand, tended to focus on action, and was primarily concerned with how the story worked, the plot's logic and legality, valuing reason and credibility. The boys found meaning in the coherence of the plot and action of the story, and defined characters by what they did rather than by any insight or change experienced by the characters. Other researchers have found a similar distinction in what boys and girls read, and in how boys and girls develop differently as a result of their upbringing, arguing that the separation and individuation of boys is a more urgent requirement for identity than it is for girls.[9]

Features of the text such as content, plot or setting also convey particular cultural values, feelings, perceptions or beliefs associated with one gender or the other. For example, the depiction of the masculine body in animations and comic representations conveys the way our society idealizes aspects of masculinity, e.g., the lack of emotional expression, the face often partially covered by a mask; the body often delineated in physically extended poses that allow a loving depiction of muscles at full stretch.[10]

Does this automatically mean, then, that boys will internalize the depictions of masculinity they find in the fantasies they enjoy? There is a danger in describing how gender is implicated in the activity of reading, of suggesting that children's gender identities are determined by social factors without the individuals themselves having any personal, active agency in their construction. This would be contrary to how we believe children actively make sense of new experience. With gender identity, as with other learning, children actively hypothesize about the meanings of their experiences, and these meanings develop over time as children first consolidate their understanding and then are challenged by wider experience to move on to more complex understandings. A more subtle explanation, therefore, implies a dynamic relationship, in which social representations of gender do indeed influence how individual children think about themselves as boys or girls, but where that subjective self-representation of gender also subverts and complicates its social representation. It is also important to remember that even young children are aware that gender is represented in multiple ways in their environment. Like their developing understanding of the linguistic register, children come to be aware that there are various discourses about gender within which they take up a range of different, often contradictory, positions.[11] In *Schoolgirl Fictions*, for instance, Valerie Walkerdine reminds us that our self-representation is not a monolithic entity: we are not 'unitary subjects uniquely positioned'.[12] We are, rather, a network of different subjectivities, depending, not only on the available positions society offers us in different contexts but also on how we rate those positions – rejecting, incorporating, or resisting them. So, when considering children's developing understanding of the social implications of their gender identity, Bronwyn Davies, in *Frogs and Snails and Feminist Tales*, describes children as *active* agents. They are able, in learning the discourses about gender expressed by their society, to position themselves selectively within the various gender practices in *multiple* ways. In doing so, they develop gender subjectivities that are both *in accordance with* and *in opposition to* the available ways in which others choose to position them.[13]

This would, of course, suggest that children who have wider experiences of other fictions and other lived narratives may have more opportunity to construct multiple identities and meanings 'against the grain' of any one narrative discourse.[14]

We need, therefore, to be mindful that children reading popular fictions may find within them something more subtle than a simple taking in of cultural indoctrination. With boys, simply deploring fighting fantasies as social 'conditioning' into a masculinity that celebrates violence as a solution to conflict might similarly miss the complexity of boys' involvements with these popular fictions. Pre-adolescent children are notably subversive of and resistant to authoritative and socially sanctioned roles and values. They test the reality of the world as mediated by adults and other sources of information about the adult world in order to reassure themselves as to the certainty of those images of the adult world in which they are about to participate in their adolescence. That reality inevitably includes ways of 'doing gender'. Reading, watching, writing and playing popular cultural masculine fantasies is a trying on of identities to see how they work in the real world. The fantasies are not only 'symptoms' of how the world works, they are also 'proposed cures' to unresolved and often unconscious dilemmas and questions facing us. One of the main unresolved questions for children, both boys and girls, involves their self-identity as effective and competent people in the adult world. In a particularly insightful essay, Gemma Moss demonstrates how the narrative of an adolescent girl reveals the uncertainty of older children entering the adult world:

> It is not the monolithic reproduction of a given order, a unitary whole, but fragmentary. It raises questions about what it might mean to leave childhood behind, to grow into womanhood and enter into relationships with men. On whose terms could this, should this, take place? What is at stake?[15]

Might boys' relationships to the warrior-fantasies offered by the adult world be equally, if differently, complex?

Learning to move freely in the world: children's desire for agency in the world

Pre-adolescence, roughly taken to describe children between the ages of 10 to 13, has been described as an age when children test the boundaries of adult-sanctioned behaviour, form close friendships and develop a finely tuned sense of how they see themselves.[16] These older children become aware of their growing independence and power, both cognitively, as they are increasingly able to organize and relate their knowledge, and effectively, as they learn to command their impulses. So, school-aged children between the ages of 10 and 12, still relatively powerless in an adult world, desire to see themselves as competent, as independent and powerful agents in the world. Often, the period of adolescence will be one in which children will be in conflict with what they also desire to be: those powerful and competent beings called parents (and sometimes teachers too).

It is not altogether surprising, then, if the fiction children enjoy at this age is mostly what can be loosely described as 'adventure fiction', in which this desire is played out in the narrative fantasy of the adventure: danger is faced and overcome, in a process whereby character is defined by struggle. Character defined by struggle seems quite an apposite way of describing the fundamental task of the pre-adolescent child, which is to begin the long enterprise of learning their way in the adult world and finding out whether they will turn out to be effective within it. In its simplest version, what children enjoy is the fantasy of competence: 'a story about having one's wish to be successful come true because of the way one skilfully acts'.[17] In the typical adventure or romance narrative, our desiring self seeks to be delivered from the anxieties of reality, but in a way that also includes and contains that reality. Pre-adolescent children's anxieties include the question of whether they are going to be competent and effective in the adult world. Adventures and romances do this, in that they contain and thus acknowledge the nature of the anxiety – threats to the self and the stable world – at the same time as they offer an assurance that these anxieties can be overcome. However, because pre-adolescent children are still quite young, they are limited in how they can imagine the conflict can be resolved. The warrior-narrative appeals because it offers a simple solution to a difficult question, one that children of this age can imagine.

In this connection I found it interesting that Liam and Dean both said they preferred computer games to TV and reading because 'you've got more control'. Perhaps the interactive nature of playing the computer game itself is incorporated into the fantasy of competence. After all, conventional reading is also a skill that has to be mastered, and most older children take delight in their competence in that skill too.

From an adult point of view, popular fictions are often thought of as irredeemably inadequate as literature. Written to formula, often by anonymous writers, the characters and plots are superficial, stereotypical and repetitive. The ideas they present about men and women are false. And yet, children read and watch these stories over and over again, role-play them with their toys and with each other, buy and collect the toys, use the dialogue in their conversations. Again and again, the heroes face slightly different versions of danger or evil or crime. And repeatedly, from episode to episode on TV, from skill-level to skill-level on the computer games, in every edition of the boys' comics, good triumphs as the heroes and heroines enact the defeat of evil. By audience figures and sales statistics, these stories are enormously popular with children.

But perhaps those criticisms of popular cultural fictions miss the developmental point. Children enjoy conventional values, polarized and stereotyped characterization, simple plots and one-sided ideals because that is the way the world looks to 10- and 11-year-olds. Or at least, that is how they have succeeded in making sense of how the world works, so far. Indeed, the repetitiveness and obsessional quality of children's involvement with these fantasies suggests why they are so attractive. In the addiction is a repeated attempt to 'assuage a confused longing, only to have it deepened'.[18] Children at this Janus-faced point in their lives are, perhaps, reassured by the fantasy of the orderliness and reliability of a world where decisions are easy, men are clearly different from women, good guys are clearly different from bad guys and conflict is resolved with a zap of the gun. Children play the fantasy over and over again at a time when it provides a secure contrast to their own rapidly changing views of the world and themselves. Like many kinds of learning, once the understanding has been exhausted, once the learning can move on, the obsessive interest wanes and the plastic warriors collect dust on the adolescent's shelf.

Perhaps it is helpful for us as teachers to remember our own reading at this age. When I began secondary school, I was very excited by the newness and difficulty of the ideas that I was learning at school and decided to join the 'adult' library, a room which I held in great awe and whose very floor polish I thought was the perfume of adulthood. I had read an article in a magazine which was one of those popular surveys of 'Who are the intellectuals of our day?' As a result, I began, aged 12, to try the hardest books I could find which, at that time, were books by de Beauvoir and Sartre! Day after day I struggled to decipher the sentences, knowing I was understanding very little of what I was reading and rather bemused by the concerns of the adults within them. In my imagination, I sat in some Parisian *boîte* with Simone de Beauvoir and considered the meaning of the Spanish Civil War and of my jealousy for one of Sartre's other lovers. After a while, my nostalgia for my childhood world became unbearable and I sneaked back to the children's library and desperately read all the *Milly-Molly-Mandy* books I could find, basking in their sunny domesticity and uncomplicated certainties. My point being that the 'trespass into adulthood' is fraught with anxieties as well as daring experimentation about one's self.

Perhaps, in the warrior-fantasies, those masked heroes enforcing the law and fighting crime and evil not only fulfil the same nostalgia for certainty but also suggest that this is how men create that certain world, and thus suggest to boys that this ideal of effective agency in the world through the physical defeat of evil is what they would aspire to? If that is so, it is nevertheless a false ideal.

There is some evidence, however, to suggest that the repetitive involvement with the fantasy leads ultimately to young readers' eventual perception of its falsity, that the image of the world offered by the adventure is unrealistic and the identity roles it offers are too simplistic.[19] In effect, they grow out of the solutions offered by the adventure genre, including the gender possibilities they portray. I offer two examples to support this suggestion.

When I started my interview with Dean and Liam, I asked them about a popular warrior-series on TV in which teenage girls and boys transform into a fighting machine and defeat or kill the enemies of world order. I offered to show them a video of this programme to cue them in to the subject. Dean and Liam began to laugh and, when I asked them if they liked the programme, they explained, apologetically, out of sympathy for my gesture, that they didn't like that programme any more. They explained that it was because 'they never lose. You know what's going to happen every week. They start getting beaten up and then they give a great big sort of "ooh look now they're going to kill you" and then they're dead. Simple.' Too simple. As the older pre-adolescent child gains wider knowledge of the world and reads more widely, the world enlarges and the ways of making sense of it which were previously sufficient are no longer so. They begin to look for stories that reflect the fact that people are not just good or bad, that there are conflicts of motive and point of view, and that the world is not so certain as we would like. This is encouraging for us as teachers. Not only can we become alert to the individual reader's growing boredom with the fantasy and encourage children to articulate their own perceptions of the inadequacy of the narrative, we can be encouraged by the fact that most boys eventually discard the fantasy as a possible template for actual living.

In the second example, Jedd finishes his story of a mother lost in the woods with the return of a father who is generous and kind. This longing, undercut by Jedd's personal joke in the sarcasm of Tom's 'exhilaratingly happy' reaction at seeing his father, led to a conventional ending which he then contradicted with a sadder but wiser knowledge of the world:

And suddenly he heard a lot of trampling and crashing of leaves. Someone was walking towards him. It was his father. Tom felt pleased and exhilaratingly happy. He had just come back from France: he was an oil-worker, and he had a lot of money and he gave Tom £20.00 to give to his mum. So his father took Tom home. Tom's mum was very pleased to see him. Next morning they got up and had a lovely big breakfast. And they lived happily ever after. (NOT REALLY!!!) [*sic*]

Jedd first dictated 'And they lived happily ever after', and I questioned it – 'Really?' Jedd looked at me wearily and said, 'Well, no not really, but that's what people want you to put at the end of stories isn't it.' When I suggested that he could say what he wanted, he decided that he very much wanted to add 'not really', and that, such was the vehemence with which he felt this, he wanted it in capitals with three exclamation marks.

'I am the Law! Drop your weapons!'

Me: Can you tell me a bit about how Terminator goes on the video game?
Barry: Well, he goes . . . Robbie, you get down here.

Robbie lies on the floor and Barry explains the story as he role-plays the thrust and parry of the warriors, with Robbie from the floor adding details to the story Barry is telling (evil people attempt to kill the Terminator and must be prevented). It ends with Robbie, a baddie, being pretend-stabbed in the eye with a big metal pole by the Terminator, the hero. Then they sit up again at the table, bright-eyed and polite year 7 pupils, in their neat uniforms, helping the lady with her research.

If the desire for competence drives the appeal of warrior fantasies for boys at this age, what kind of competence do they suggest is appropriate for men? Warrior narratives appear to be mostly plot: the emphasis is on fast-moving action in which a series of repetitive fighting episodes is interrupted by suspenseful climaxes which eventually lead to a conclusive confrontation. Often, a journey or a change of setting is involved. Character is formulaic or sketchy and the narratives borrow heavily from folk and legend sources, sometimes translated into contemporary equivalents. There are supernatural agents such as wise elders, magicians, witches. Other features of warrior-narratives include the transformation of the human into something else (machine or beast) and anthropomorphic treatments – animals who can talk and intelligent pet creatures who can show the way, warn, etc. In the computer games, as elsewhere, heroes collect magic talismans – often quite arbitrary in their symbolic form – and all heroes have magical weapons, from swords to missile launchers or even a superhuman body that is used as a weapon or which sometimes literally turns into a 'fighting-machine', as in films like *Terminator* and *Robocop*. There are also the many articulated warrior figures and transformer toys that can be manipulated from human shape to become weapons and transporters.[20]

In the popular culture the boys refer to, justice and the law act as central plot devices. The enemies are almost invariably evil agents of injustice and the warrior-hero's task is to prevent their success generally by physical defeat and to bring about a return to a just society, one which looks very like current American society in its idealized form. Conflict is resolved through the physical defeat of these enemies of the law. In one popular version of this theme an American-speaking, fatherly disembodied head guides the actions of the superheroes. As such, it is a visual signal of the unquestioned and superordinate 'law' that provides the justification for the heroes' violent behaviour.

On the TV, in the narrative of some computer games and in generic videos and films such as *Terminator, Demolition Man* and *Robocop*, violence and destruction become legitimate 'because they are presented as necessary means for halting the violence already initiated by the men and monsters who have threatened the social order'.[21] It is argued that this is replicated in society in that male violence is often explained by its perpetrators as people having stepped out of line, upsetting the social order by not remaining in their role, thus challenging the social *status quo*, challenging the position and identity of the aggressor. Therefore, it is the aggressor who is threatened and who has to use violence to restore order.[22]

I watch Dean twist the plastic in his hands, transforming the toy from man to weapon, talking in an absorbed whispered tone:

This one's called Sumo-Box. It's got like a missile on one hand and a proper hand, got proper feet and it's got a recharger here and you press that and it charges up, same with this one here – he's got a great big claw – he's got a recharger and he changes into a helicopter [demonstrates] . . . and he's got boosters on the back of his feet.

The computer games and video films the boys played with and watched were almost always about men (except for the *Home Alone* films); boys did not feature in any of the other film narratives; Robbie and Barry act out the violent and warlike actions of men, not boys. Seeking to know how to be an adult, boys find access to the world of men through media representations. 'Film, television and comics provide armatures on which boys can wind all kinds of fantasy' and provide structures which amount to 'boyhood rituals of entry into manhood'.[23] Superman, for example, gives boys an idealized image of what they dream of being when they become adults.[24] However, the popular fictions enjoyed by boys rarely show boys learning how to carry out adult tasks. They are not educative about human relations, as girls' fictions tend to be, nor are they subtle about emotions. Men in boys' popular fictions are strong and they fight other men when they get angry. (They also, increasingly, fight women.) But there is no place for boys in those fictions, and no way to read about how to be an effective agent in negotiating the transition into the adult male's world. What often occurs instead is the magical 'transformation' of weak humanity to hypermasculinity: Clark Kent to Superman, 'ordinary teenagers' to supernaturally powerful warriors, and boys to men.

Adult men write and draw, direct and act in these popular fictions. It is their fantasies, their images and their ideas which are offered to boys. For example, Pat Mills and John Wagner, the creators of Judge Dredd, explain: 'Dredd was going to be the adolescent reader's nightmare, a strict character of non-forgiveness, a severe father-figure who was always right and always on top.'[25] As such, Judge Dredd was what men thought boys might be assumed both to most fear and most aspire to become. The authors thought the fantasy of Judge Dredd would give their young readership 'the unique thrill of seeing your deepest fears and darkest wishes enacted at the same time'.

So, I find that pre-adolescent children have a developmental task which is mirrored in the popular culture that they enjoy.

In mastering that task, they have recourse, amongst other adult models and messages, to the texts of competence offered in the toys, TV programmes, computer games and films they enjoy. Those fantasies come in gender-specific forms and so tie in to the child's desire to represent themselves as competent by linking this to representations of masculine or feminine identity. However, for most children, it is not a case of simply 'catching' the genre and applying it to real life so much as providing a 'good enough' explication of their understanding and a 'satisfactory enough' resolution to their anxieties, until such time as their experience and understanding develops further and they move beyond them.

The danger lies when there is no movement through the fantasy to other possibilities. For example, some research indicates that where there is no belief in one's ability to overcome fate, children's own warrior-fantasies do not develop beyond a plot in which escape from danger occurs but the original threat continues to exist. Perhaps those children who come to expect to fail in school and whose social and cultural environments suggest they have no power to change their circumstances out of school, might find themselves particularly locked into the seductiveness of warrior-fantasies, forever policing the world for transgressions against their self-image. In this connection, studies of young violent men have also observed that there is an element of quasi-paranoia about their defence and defensiveness of the self against possible transgressions by others.

What *Flannan Isle* meant to Jedd

Reading is, as we know, an interaction between a particular reader and a particular text in a particular time and place: the narrative is incomplete until it is read. The reader brings to the text her or his expectations based on experience of life and of other texts, while the text itself also contains the author's socially and historically located assumptions about life and other texts. It is in the meeting of these worlds that meanings are forged. The activity of reading is also a social activity in itself; its significance varies according to the social context in which it occurs. For children, reading usually occurs at school or at home; with an adult (or sanctioned by adults), with a group of friends or on their own; and in the particular socio-economic and cul-

tural communities to which they belong. In these different contexts, what children read, what they read for and their feelings
about the activity vary. For example, 12-year-old Jedd, claiming
falsely to be unable to read and write in school, and an avowed
'hater' of stories, dictates a story in which a boy loses his mother
in the forest. The boy in the story is scared. We talk about
feeling scared, and then Jedd goes back to the story. The boy is
scared, Jedd decides, because there are wolves in the forest.

Jedd: Put 'He started calling his mum's name.'

IU: What? He called her 'Norah' or 'Mum'?

Jedd: Er, yeah, 'Mum'.

IU: Do you want me to put that in speech marks?

Jedd: Go on then, with a capital . . . all in capitals though,
because he's shouting.

IU: What, like that?

Jedd: Mm . . . [long pause] 'He couldn't find his mum
anywhere.'

IU: Right.

Jedd: Do you know what I just thought of? . . . did you ever
read *Flannan Isle*?

IU: Yes.

Jedd: I think I've got it in my bag [scrabbles in giant sports
bag].

IU: Have you?

Jedd: Yeah, it's a really cool thing . . . right? That just reminded
me of it because certain things, you know, where people keep
dying and stuff like that.

Jedd, soon to be expelled for persistent violence and disruptive behaviour in the school, brings his personal life and its
insecurities to a reading of *Flannan Isle* that makes it a significant
experience for him. The ballad gains its meaning in this particular reading within Jedd's own contingency. Furthermore, he was,
I suspect, only able to share his experience of vulnerability in
the particular context of a teacher sitting down and scribing his
own stories without judgement on content or style. The meanings of this intimate context allowed different discourses, different relations to occur between Jedd and a 'grup', as he referred
to grown-ups. Even the scrabbling in the big sports bag is part
of the significance of this act of reading – Jedd wanted to own
his photocopy of this poem, when all the other bits of paper he

was given in school were regarded as unwanted and resented impositions and were soon lost. Somehow it was important to find the actual text and show it to me. I interpreted this as an unusual act of trust, since what he was showing me was that he was moved by the poem's depiction of abandonment and desolation. Unluckily, Jedd's frictionless surface to school learning had worked only too well and he had lost that text too.

Jedd showed me that, contrary to school's expectations of him, he experienced a sense of loss and vulnerability that was only possible for us to talk about within the framework of fiction and within a particular kind of relationship between teacher and pupil. It emphasized yet again that narrative and fiction comment upon and deepen children's most profound and barely conscious experiences. Similarly, with Terry, I scribed a long, long narrative of death and despair, with blood streaming down walls and children left impaled on spikes, that was derived from all the video films he had been watching. Unlike Jedd, he could not talk outside the dictation of the narrative, but was both the pursuer and the pursued within the violent fiction. Finally, the evil character seemed to be vanquished. But the confusion of identity did not end there: Terry, the victim, was 'sentenced to seven months' therapy' because the police did not believe him. 'So that was the end of Freddie – or was it?' While he was lying in his bed, Terry-the-aggressor reappeared, in the form of blood streaming down his wall.

It is not that we as teachers have to be able to psychoanalyse these stories so much as to respect that what happens in the interaction between popular fiction and boys involves crises and anxieties about identity itself. Boys themselves are exploring, directly and indirectly, through their responses to those narratives (e.g., how they write their own versions, how they free-associate, like Jedd, on the relationship between their lives and the fictions they read), the limitations and dangers of the gender roles they are offered by society. Perhaps in these extreme examples, we can begin to find reasons why the superwarrior fantasy is so seductive for young boys.

SECTION 2: READING AS A SHARED SOCIAL PRACTICE

Tony: *Home Alone 2*, yeah ... Well, he's on ... the MacAlisters are going on a holiday, yeah, and he's left in the house. And the people are going to get him. So he does all these tricks and all that.

[Tony, Kieron, and Andy all start to talk at once, describing the actions, acting them out, developing and contradicting each other's utterances.]

Andy: You don't know!

Tony: When they opened the door, they all, their hand was on fire. And then, that was one of the tricks. And then, after they'd run up stairs, they had all marbles, marbles and they tripped over. And then on the stairs when they were climbing up, they had three tins, three tins and there was a massive steel bar and the three tins come along. 'Missed!' [American accent]. Another one comes along. 'Missed!' And then the kid goes out and, 'Do you reckon you can get me now?' And then the big steel bar comes along and bangs them right on the head and they fell down [mimes being hit on the head and staggering].

Andy (prompting the next part of the story):   And then they fall through the floorboards.

Kieron (ignoring the prompt):   I like the bit when he goes 'Hey, are you in there?' and he gets this staple gun and he goes [shooting noises] and he goes [pain and agony noises].

Me: I didn't quite get that.

Tony: Well they put a shotgun with a pin in the end and . . . yeah, he put his head through the cat's thing.

Andy: Weren't a real shotgun, you know.

Tony: I know. You know the cat flap? He gets his shoe stuck in it. So he pulls it out and he puts his head through there and sees where it's gone. And Macauley Calkins shots the shotgun. 'Hello!' [in mocking voice].

Kieron (to me):   Can I do one now? . . . Has anyone done *Mask*, yeah?

Children share popular culture far more than they do the traditionally solitary activity of reading. Most of the boys I spoke to read very little out of school (mostly football magazines, but there's another story), but when they did it was usually at bedtime or in their bedrooms during the day. In interaction with their peer group, children actively interpret the symbols and content of the popular culture they engage with. It is argued that by doing this they appropriate the media content into their larger social worlds. I would want to argue that this is a process of collaborative learning and that groups of boys may also pass through this learning to wider and deeper understandings rather than the implication that collaborative peer talk amongst pre-adolescents is socially determining. Crucially, the models of older boys are a significant source of information as to alternative possibilities. Again, it rather depends on the boys' other circumstances, such as their social class, domestic stability, religious and ethnic values and their individual personal development. However, because media has the power to mass-produce a manufactured public world, children's social interactions, in the playground, in non-adult discourse, in the TV series-related toys they buy and discuss with each other, do, however temporarily, produce and reproduce larger cultural patterns, such as the social practices that we identify as masculine or feminine.[26]

Pre-adolescent children are able to develop, to some extent, a society of their own which lies outside the watchful gaze of the adults who care for and teach them. In their private society they can learn the collective informal wisdom about the culture and about social relationships as practised in the world beyond the family and the school. They can also, importantly, explore deviance from and subversion of adult values, knowingly behaving in ways that lie outside the rules of the adult world, as well as rehearsing, often in exaggerated form, the roles and fantasies that will influence their adult roles.

Collaborative talk amongst pre-adolescent boys is characterized by utterances that are taken up, supported and ratified by the other boys in the group in a process that builds group cohesiveness and solidarity. The use of 'embellishment' (exaggeration) in the discourse is a key process which acts as an intensifier, indicating the salient meanings children want to emphasize.

Tony, Kieron and Andy were artificially grouped together for the purposes of my interview with them. Being in a room with a strange woman inevitably impaired the authenticity of the discourse. Pre-adolescent boys, for example, spend a great deal of time and energy rehearsing behaviour that would not be sanctioned by parents and teachers, e.g., aggressiveness, both verbally, through insults, pranks and dares, as well as physically, in mock attacks and play fights.[27] On the whole, they try to shield adults from this deviant behaviour. The pupils I talked to undoubtedly engaged in some self-censorship, as became particularly evident when they wanted to talk about sexual scenes in films they enjoyed. Nevertheless, it is evident that the boys I spoke to knew and expected the discourse to be shared amongst them, even when they found managing that process a little difficult in the presence of adults.

Tony, Kieron and Andy used repetition and the prolonging of favoured images, actions, discourses from mass media by repeated imitations of verbal routines and actions, as well as affirming these with laughter and assents ('yeah') to intensify the meanings that were important in their peer culture. The importance of detailed accuracy, in terms of remembering exact lines, tones of voice, particularly communicative poses and actions, is clearly evident in the dialogue quoted above. Andy, in particular, takes on the role of accuracy-monitor, e.g., 'Weren't a real shotgun, you know'.

Four themes predominated in Milkie's[28] boys' social discourse about mass media, none likely to be sanctioned by the adult world: talk about sexuality, especially aggressive sexuality; bodily functions; violence; and drug and alcohol use. She particularly emphasizes that, of these themes, the two that are central to the reproduction of the male role are aggression, including aggressive sexuality, and violence. In my interviews with Robbie and Barry, and with Tony, Andy and Kieron, there was an unembarrassed relish of violent scenes. Robbie and Barry explained how they reacted when watching violent videos. If they were watching with other people, sometimes they discreetly looked away if it was in slow motion or dwelt on the 'gruesomeness', to use Dean's word. Otherwise, you had to 'take it', i.e., just watch and try not to be affected. Sexual scenes could be embarrassing if your little brother was there with you. I asked them if they liked violence. 'Oh, yes!' they replied, enthusiastically, smiling brightly at me, and Robbie described how his father had shown him a way of kicking someone 'where it hurts' if he got into a fight. It is hard to give a context to Robbie's remarks that would not lead the reader to pathologize him. He was from a working-class family who were known to the school for domestic difficulties, and he did get into fights at school. Nevertheless, he worked in his lessons, and was helpful and polite around the school. He was not unusually aggressive or antagonistic to school, but he was proud to let me know that he knew members of the notorious fighting families in the town. Is it part of *my* pathology that I did not regard his remarks as shocking or extreme?

The children I talked to in another school also referred to sexually aggressive scenes with enthusiasm:

> when Freddie, Freddie Kruger's ... this lady is in the shower having a nice shower and Freddie comes up behind her on the wall he goes [noises] and he goes [noises] ... yeah, and he rips her neck out. Then he goes [noises]. You can see her heart beating, right?

Sexual talk among Milkie's boys was common and explicit, and she notes in particular the language (as well as the gestures) in which they begin to elide the narration of fictional character ('he') and their imagining themselves ('I/you') and embodying themselves in the role:

Matt: And that other guy, he goes ... he goes [pumping his hand in the air] 'Aah, aah, cut the bullshit', an' he goes [mimes lifting a woman's skirt and gyrates his hips in a copulation imitation] [laughter].

Paul: Man, that woman was asleep there, and she's sleepin' [puts arm behind his head] like this. Now how could you handle it?

Matt: ... how about when he didn't know ... he goes ... she goes [mimes ripping off a shirt], 'Take me', and I go, 'Yeah!' [giggles].

Paul: Man, did you see that one thing – it was [cupping hands at his chest] an' was [indicating large bust].[29]

Through these collaborative linguistic processes of embellishment, the boys collectively negotiate meaning, which includes gendered meaning. Gender themes, in fact, predominate in frequency and intensity in pre-adolescent boys' peer culture. According to Milkie, the ability to carry on a discourse of sex and violence 'acts as a marker for successfully presenting oneself as achieving peer competence'.[30] The themes are particularly necessary to boys' attempts to present themselves as masculine and to demonstrate to each other that they were men. From popular culture portrayals of men's behaviour, they gleaned their perceptions of masculine roles and identities. Being tough and aggressive was defined as meaningful and was highly valued. Being capable of talking in a sexually knowledgeable way, if not yet able to indulge in the older adolescent's 'phallic brag' of competence and/or experience, was also important. Challenges to one's sexuality through insults and teases about one's homosexuality or femaleness were common.

Somehow, the description of a pre-adolescent's peer culture suggests that trying out media images of masculine identities becomes amplified in the boys' collaborative talk. This suggests that social learning occurs that works to conceal boys' private vulnerabilities which popular culture did in fact address. In order to find out if the media images of masculinity work, boys have to try them out on each other. It is in this process that a *public* discourse of masculinity begins to be formed. Thus, it is not the reading of popular culture itself that leads to the formation of particular masculine identities, but what the boys take from it in social interaction with their peers. What may be significant for consideration here is the idea of investment. What pay-off is there for boys to engage in this glorification of aggression and violence, which uses the images and narratives of popular culture? It seems to me that pre-adolescent boys are particularly vulnerable and isolated at this point in their journey into manhood, and that mass images of manhood provide a spurious universality that can be used by boys to feel part of a peer culture that gives them some security. The groups also allow a discourse to occur that is disapproved of by adults. It is therefore also a place where reality can be tested by trying on extreme identities and seeing how they work and what their limitations are. What I want to resist is the suggestion that these conversations are part of a determining process, which boys cannot choose but internalize and which leads directly to their later behaviour as men in their real lives. It is in the developmental argument that I find some optimism. As the children become older, they become more self-aware, and more interested in realism, and these processes lead them to be able to take more individual decisions and to seek the greater complexity of realistic images of manhood. Perhaps teachers can be ready to encourage these processes as individuals seem to tire of their pre-adolescent involvement in the warrior-fantasy.

SECTION 3: THE SCHOOL'S RESPONSE

Liam and Dean don't like reading in school. They sit at the front near the teacher's desk (my teacher-self can guess why) and they say that, during reading time, all the other kids, when they go up to read to the teacher, jog their elbows or make the books fly out of their hands. This reading just won't stay still! Anyway, Liam slyly concedes, he doesn't really read the books, he looks through a book to confirm that it's going to be boring and then goes through a pretence of book-choosing behaviour, repeating this process until reading time is up. Sometimes the books are not boring, but he and Dean are somewhat outraged by the deceitfully attractive covers put on books to make you want to read them and then, when you look inside, well, they're boring again! I try to pursue (all my teaching life, it seems) *why* they find these books boring. Dean, in tones expressive of the utter predictability of it all, drawls in a sing-song voice the story-grammar's setting, and the emphasis on relationship: 'It's just about . . . they're walking around seeing other people. "Oh hi! How are *you*? Oh we *are* having *fun*!" ' He then parodies the banality of the narrative in the story-grammar's attempt to introduce surprising events and a conflict: 'And then the next day they go along and there's somebody else in *town*!' Dean enacts the conflict and challenge to identity/power in the most pared-down dialogue possible:

'Who are you?'
'I'm the coolest guy in town.'
Then there'll be like have an argument about like: 'I'm the best man in town.'
'No, I am.'

[This tails off into muttered repetitions of the statement of conflict.]

'I am' . . .' 'no, I am' . . . 'I am . . .' 'no, I am . . .'

[Then Liam, who seems to have a really well-developed sensitivity to the boringness of reading, elaborates in his best tones of contempt, the adult moral intentions in the book revealed in the resolution of the narrative.]

'And at the end they like make up and go, "Oooh! we ought to have been friends all along!" '

[Dean reiterates.]

'or "Oh dear! we've been such *fools* to be *arguing*! Oh! Oh *gosh*!" '

Dean and Liam's reaction to school reading warns us that attempts to broaden the repertoire on which they can draw to construct understandings about masculinity are not always successful. Simply providing more socially acceptable texts only confirms for Dean and Liam that schools are boring places where reading is work and is to be avoided wherever possible. Sadly, schools seem so often to turn the pleasure of reading into reading which is work. Gradually, as children move through primary and into secondary school, fiction becomes something to pay close attention to and analyse, and as the priority in school reading becomes more and more turned to the factual, we communicate our own dismissal of 'just' fantasy as somehow babyish or indulgent or as poor preparation for adult life. For many children school offers dull reading and dull ways of reading it.

We are often encouraged to help children to read 'against the grain' of the books, where that leads to resistance to the representations of gender that are being placed on them. But Dean and Liam clearly are already reading 'against the grain': perhaps against our wishes, they use parody and satire to remain resistant to the adult blandishments they detect in the books they read at school – to resolve conflict amicably and find interest in relationships. And thus, they remain resistant to the implied school critiques of the fantasies of masculinity they construct in their popular fictions outside school.

What then can we do to encourage boys like Dean and Liam to consider other types of competence and other forms of power than those glamorized in the warrior-narrative? How will Dean and Liam develop what they can take from their reading of popular culture and their reading in school?

Perhaps our first strategy as teachers would be to develop our own empathetic understanding and entry into the power of the popular fantasies of masculinity for the boys we teach and to find a way that brings those popular fictions within school in a way that does not 'emasculate' them. To do this would be, as Lacan points out, to bring to light 'the manifestation of the subject's desire'. This would mean, I believe, teachers opening themselves to reflecting imaginatively on the stories' meanings. In this way, the teacher's role is to understand and indeed enter into the logic of the boys' points of view rather than attempting to simply efface or eradicate them. In addition, we would need to be conscious of how stories may have different force for individual boys, speaking not only to the large social groupings they may belong to, but also to their individual circumstances within their cultural settings, and their individual developmental progress, cognitively, affectively and as a reader. Perhaps we can, to some extent, be reassured by the implications of the developmental argument. Children may become deeply involved with the warrior-fictions because at that particular stage of their cognitive and affective development such narratives represent their understanding of the way the world works and provide an assimilable model of how to be competent and effective within it. Perhaps the second thing we can do, then, is to allow children the time and the experiences necessary to consolidate the knowledge and understanding to be gained from this stage of their reading experience. During that time, we could also develop our own understanding of what boys might be gaining that is of value from these popular fictions by observing and letting boys talk to us about how they use these narratives outside school, thus incorporating and giving recognition to those experiences within schooling. From specific dialogues with actual boys we teach, we can learn also how to offer ourselves as experienced readers, able to model how to read and talk about books, showing ways of comparing and evaluating what we read. We can help them to make connections between favourite narratives, whether in popular culture or in previous school reading, and new books, so that their shared reading world, one they can talk to each other about, is continually reorganized and reabsorbed.

Thus, we could avoid the educational moralizing that is clearly so counterproductive.[31] For pre-adolescent and adolescent children, adult disapproval, however 'rational' its argument, may simply further legitimize their semi-subversive stance towards institutional values. As Jordan points out, for the 'fighting boys', masculinity is constructed partly around resistance to perceived school expectations.[32] This supports Willis's argument about how working-class 'lads' inverted the values of school to construct their own definition of masculinity.[33] Messages from the teacher of her or his disapproval of the popular fictions boys enjoy may therefore be received as desirable confirmations of the child's fantasies about masculinity.

And yet, as teachers, we often feel called upon to resist or oppose the power of mass media and popular fictions. Teachers are rightly concerned to help children gain mastery over the powerful gender stereotypes that are learned at least partly through the popular culture they enjoy and communicate with each other. I conclude that we must intervene but, as Williamson points out, this cannot be done by teaching children 'about' gender without also asking children to examine their own experience. This requires a level of inward thinking and aware-ness of other points of view that may only be possible among older students. It can also be quite threatening for children to be expected to display their personal experience if the gaze of adult teachers in school represents for some children an alienat-ing authority that disregards and diminishes the meaningfulness of their out-of-school experiences and desires.

It has also been suggested that we could encourage boys to detach the desire for identity inherent in the warrior-fantasy from the model of an aggressive masculine hero and to encour-age its attachment to more admirable and fulfilling masculinit-ies.[34] Jordan[35] gives the example of a woman teacher (possessing unusual levels of credibility for the primary school-aged boys in her class, I would imagine) telling them that, 'Real men can walk away from fights.' Another approach, which is related to this suggestion and, as far as I am concerned, more workable, is to introduce boys to other fictions that embody the same narrative desire for competence and effectiveness in the world and which offer masculine models of heroism and courage, but which add complexity of character and plot, and grace of lan-guage to the experience. Narratives such as the *Iliad* or drama such as *Macbeth*, unlike the pseudo-literature parodied by Dean and Liam, deepen the meaning of the warrior-narrative in ways that may lead boys to see both its limitations and how it applies in other representations of masculinity. As *Active Approaches to Shakespeare* have shown, primary-aged children can understand and work with apparently 'difficult' texts, if we are willing and imaginative. The great advantage is that the activity remains within the fictional world of metaphor, where children can make sense of their narratives of desire.

What seem to turn some children away from reading are books that deny the pleasures of fantasy and bring children back to contemplating the everyday. What they seem to love, and desire, are fantasies of self-reliant children. Even today, even in compre-hensive schools serving mostly working-class girls and boys, books such as *The Secret Garden* and *The Children of Green Knowe* and authors such as Robert Westall or Margaret Mahy continue to capture the imaginations of both boys and girls, tap into the narrative desires of children making sense of new worlds, new environments and also of their own self-representations. I would add that an almost essential ingredient is that these books are read *to* children, not used as 'reading practice'; that they are mediated through what most teachers do brilliantly, which is to read stories so that they come alive and to communicate their own love of the story so that teller and listener share, in the telling, the pleasure of the text. Teaching about the text may follow, but first has to come the mutuality of the pleasure of the narrative. Later, comparisons can be made that draw children's attention to the similarities between popular cultural narratives and the new texts they read and listen to in school, and that help them to begin thinking about why those particular meanings – journeys, tests, magic, heroes and heroines – seem to continue to appear in stories from earliest times to the latest computer games.

Further, if both boys' and girls' narratives are narratives of competence, children can be encouraged to look at texts as similar in that respect and to look at what is *common* to girls' and boys' narratives of desire, as well as how they differ, and through this to draw attention to why the differences are related to how girls and boys learn about competence in the world. In classrooms where attention is paid to the equal opportunities for girls, these very practices of giving girls a voice may also act as a new and challenging framework in which boys have to *think about* their assumptions about being a boy becoming a man.

We know that boys in particular also pursue the narrative of competence and agency through non-fiction, learning about the world through information books and instruction manuals and lists. Again, models of masculinity are involved in reading about the world. Many boys who could not read very well would bring me large books about angling or cars or football skills that they absolutely wanted to read and which spoke to them of an adult masculine world that was just as important to them as fantasies of dominance and superiority. Often these were books from home, and often these were homes without many books, particularly fiction. Dads and step-dads, uncles, grandads and big brothers would take them fishing or to drag racing or they played in local Sunday league football. These were other models of masculinity that boys wanted to know about. Often for the first time, they saw a use for reading in making them more competent, not just as readers but as effective and competent to enter the adult masculine world. For many adult readers, and especially it would seem, for men, 'how things work' is still a particularly enjoyable reason to read, even with fiction.

Another factor of complexity that we might consider is that children of this age become adept at parody – hence their great enjoyment of comedy and comics on television that 'take off' aspects of everyday life. This is demonstrated in their references to individual comedians and comedy programmes. Children take on and act out the characteristics and the language of parodic comic characters as much as they do warriors. It seems to me that this subversion of adult and institutional values and the parodies they offer contains the seeds of what boys' resistance might be like if we can find a way for boys to harness it to a deconstruction of the warrior-narrative.

Importantly, it is in children's writing that children may develop their own deepening understanding of the warrior-narrative and explore its territory and boundaries. In drafting and redrafting, in conferencing with boys, and with girls, as well as with adult teachers, in experimenting with the genre and turning it upside down, playing with its characteristics and characterizations, children recapitulate, reflect and revise their narrative desire. Here is the prime location where personal narrative meaning is being formulated and where it is open to contestation. The teacher's sensitivity to what the child needs the story for is essential here in order to learn from the child, rather than impose new narratives. The child's narrative requires, not a 'revised telling' from the teacher but an imaginative reflection, a dialogue of response like listening to music or looking at painting.

Where Terry was totally in the grip of his narrative it would have been pointless to have directed his attention elsewhere. But it was just possible to ask him to reflect on what it meant to him to construct that story. At the end of his hunted, whirlwind, domination by dictation ('put this . . . write this . . . let's get on with it'), in a brief moment when we were able to talk more equally, he answered my question about whether he felt like the boy who ran away from Freddie or like Freddie himself, by deciding that he felt like both. What better resolution to that terror of powerlessness and the desire of total domination than the solution of the warrior-fantasy? Terry, it transpired, was a haemophiliac who found the need to be careful physically and to worry about his very corporal identity and mortality desperately frustrating. He deliberately teased children in school to hit him and would throw himself off PE equipment. I imagine that somewhere in his consciousness he was also very frightened by his condition. In his story, death stalks and blood streams and there is no final resolution. It felt more important to let Terry use fantasy to articulate these thoughts *at that stage of his progress* and to see them outside himself on the page, where he could read and reread them, playing over the meanings of his fears and desires, than to hurry him along the educational road to 'better' literature and 'finer' writing.

On the other hand, Jedd, standing on the boundary of the dark wood of adolescence, turns and says 'Not really', like a final wave goodbye to a previous world of certainties, of easy characterizations into the 'goodies' and 'baddies' that Dean and Liam refer to without irony and to the triumph of good over evil by magical heroes. And indeed, Dean and Liam themselves are beginning to find the warrior-narrative too simple an explanation: 'They never lose. It's always the same.' Here, too, the teacher's timing and sensitivity to these cues is important and requires a response tuned to individual differences if the teacher is to acknowledge and bring to the children's own awareness the meanings of their boredom and loss of interest – why the story cannot always end 'happily ever after', and why heroes who never lose no longer satisfy. From this point, the teacher can encourage children to write new narratives – sometimes subversive, sometimes parodic, sometimes tentative new explorations: to share with boys new and authentic fictional experiences that offer wider and newer possibilities and other models of narrative, to encourage their more self-aware and cognitive capacity to think about one's thinking by engaging them critically with the structure and effects of popular culture. By working *with* boys' experiences, boys' desires for competence and self-representations as masculine, by accepting levels of meaning and understanding that go beyond instrumental parallelism between fiction and reality, by showing interest and creativity in how we ourselves understand boys' absorption in the popular culture and its warrior-fantasies; perhaps in these ways we may succeed in helping boys to widen their repertoire of narratives, consider the gaps and slippages between different texts and their real lives, so that their needs and experiences are not excluded from school, where learning is, as it should be, related to the understanding and development of the real desires that frame their lived experience.

NOTES

*With acknowledgements to Dean and Liam, Robbie and Barry, Terry and Jedd, Andy, Tony and Kieron.
 1 Heath, S. B. (1983) *Ways with Words: Language, Life and Work in Communities and Classrooms*, Cambridge: Cambridge University Press.
 2 Fox, C. (1993) *At the Very Edge of the Forest: The Influence of Literature on Storytelling by Children*, London: Cassell; Brooks, P. (1992) *Reading for the Plot: Design and Intention in Narrative*, Boston, Mass.: Harvard University Press; Appleyard, J. A. (1991) *Becoming a Reader: The Experience of Fiction from Childhood to Adulthood*, Cambridge: Cambridge University Press.
 3 Willis, P. (1977) *Learning to Labour: How Working-class Kids get Working-class Jobs*, Farnborough: Saxon House.
 4 Appleyard, op. cit., p. 59.
 5 Connell, J. W. (1986) *Gender and Power: Society, the Person and Sexual Politics*, Sydney: Allen & Unwin, p. 183.
 6 Radway, J. (1984) *Reading the Romance: Women, Patriarchs and Popular Literature*, Capel Hill, N.C.: University of North Carolina Press; Moss, G. (1993) 'The Place for Romance in Young People's Writing' in Christian-Smith, L. K. (ed.) *Texts of Desire: Essays on Fiction, Femininity and Schooling*, Lewes: The Falmer Press.
 7 Jordan, E. (1995) 'Fighting Boys and Fantasy Play: The Construction of Masculinity in the Early Years of School' *Gender and Education*, Vol. 7, No. 1.
 8 Cherland, M. R. (1994) *Private Practices: Girls Reading Fiction and Constructing Identity*, London: Taylor & Francis.
 9 Appleyard, op. cit., p. 92; Chodorow, N. (1978) *The Reproduction of Mothering: Psychoanalysis and the Sociology of Gender*, Berkeley, Calif.: University of California Press.
10 Middleton, P. (1992) *The Inward Gaze: Masculinity and Subjectivity in Modern Culture*, London: Routledge.
11 Moore, H. (1994) 'The Problem of Explaining Violence' in Harvey, P. and Gow, P. (eds) *Sex and Violence: Issues in Representation and Experience*, London: Routledge.
12 Walkerdine, V. (1990) *Schoolgirl Fictions*, London: Verso.

13 Davies, B. (1989) *Frogs and Snails and Feminist Tales: Preschool Children and Gender*, Sydney: Allen & Unwin.
14 Christian-Smith, L. K. (1993) (ed.) *Texts of Desire: Essays on Fiction, Femininity and Schooling*, London: The Falmer Press.
15 Moss, op. cit.
16 Fine, G. A. and Sandstrom, K. L. (1988) *Knowing Children: Participant Observation with Minors*, London: Sage; Appleyard, op. cit.
17 Appleyard, op. cit.
18 Mason, B. A. (1975) in Appleyard, op. cit.
19 Appleyard, op. cit.
20 Appleyard, op. cit.
21 Middleton, op. cit., pp. 29–30.
22 Moore, op. cit.
23 Middleton, op. cit., p. 23.
24 Middleton, op. cit., p. 40.
25 Jarman, C. M. and Acton, P. (1995) *Judge Dredd: the Mega-History*, Lennard Publishing.
26 Milkie, M. A. (1994) 'Social World Approach to Cultural Studies: Mass Media and Gender in the Adolescent Peer Group' *Journal of Contemporary Ethnography*, Vol. 23, No. 3, October.
27 Fine and Sandstrom, op. cit.
28 Milkie, op. cit., pp. 272–3.
29 Milkie, op. cit.
30 Milkie, op. cit.
31 Williamson, J. (1981/2) 'How Does Girl Number Twenty Understand Ideology?' *Screen Education*, 40, Autumn–Winter.
32 Jordan, op. cit.
33 Willis, op. cit.
34 Paley, V. G. (1984) *Boys and Girls: Superheroes in the Doll Corner*, Chicago, Il.: University of Chicago Press.
35 Jordan, op. cit.

FURTHER READING

Texts of Desire: Essays on Fiction, Femininity and Schooling (edited by Linda K. Christian-Smith, The Falmer Press, 1993)
These essays stimulate with their various perspectives of girls' reading in their teens, and how these very popular texts are linked with desire and fantasy as well as with politics and social representations of gender. In particular, I found the essays by Gemma Moss and Bronwyn Davies particularly grounded in young women's experiences and theoretically powerfully argued.

Private Practices: Girls Reading Fiction and Constructing Identity (Meredith Rogers Cherland, Taylor & Francis, 1994)
Meredith Cherland's anthropological study is an engrossing examination of some middle-class girls' fictional reading in the contexts of school and their home community, which demonstrates how gender

is culturally and socially constructed and how literacy is involved in reproducing those social practices. She makes powerful suggestions for radical pedagogical responses that would lead to social transformations in how boys and girls represent themselves.

Despite both these texts having a focus in girls' reading experiences, the issues and debates raise challenging questions for thinking about boys' reading practices. Both give up-to-date analyses of the theoretical arguments which will lead our thinking forward about subjectivity, texts and desire.

Becoming a Reader: The Experience of Fiction from Childhood to Adulthood (J. A. Appleyard, S.J., Cambridge University Press, 1991)
This readable and even-handed book attempts to make use of psychological theories of cognitive development and psychodynamic theories of affective development to produce a description of reading which attempts to integrate processes of cognitive, affective and social development. As such, it differs in its analysis and conclusions from the post-structural analyses which tend to frame the feminist discussions above.

The Inward Gaze: Masculinity and Subjectivity in Modern Culture (Peter Middleton, Routledge, 1992)
A thoughtful and movingly argued account of men's subjectivity that includes reflections on the meaning of boyhood. The book contains lively descriptions of boys' superhero comics as well as later theorizing about the sexual politics of emotion.

Epilogue

Mary Hilton

INTELLECTUAL GROWTH

Throughout this book we have gathered and displayed evidence of children busily engaged with texts. In Chapter 1 I focused on children's imaginative play with toy figures which the toy industry sells in order to extend the possibilities of video narratives. Often children are affectively engaged with powerful story videos as David Whitley and Helen Bromley show in Chapters 2 and 3. Throughout their lives children are bedding down layers of meaning, switching positions and registers, as Cathy Pompe discusses in Chapter 4. And Gill Venn and Isobel Urquhart show in Chapters 5 and 6 different groups of boys and girls deeply engaged with the texts of popular culture as they attempt to cross over into adulthood. Throughout these studies we see evidence of children's active and emotional responses to texts which have reached them from an industry outside school and we describe how they use these texts to give themselves pleasure. Throughout the book the authors suggest how and why this pleasure is constructed and 'read' and suggest how this might lead to classroom practices where these texts are understood *from the inside*, showing the grain of desire operating within the growing consciousness of individual children. In addition, we have shown how the intense gendering of the popular culture industry for children is also read and used by growing children, giving them texts and messages about their bodies which, we argue, they will need to integrate in order to achieve mature and stable adult subjectivity. The industry, through its narratives and images, sets out differing areas of male and female competence, which again children enjoy, delighting in the adult power this seems to suggest and using the different narratives to build their own play of desire.

We have suggested that in a sensitive classroom, where a model of literacy is developed which works with the growth of individual consciousness, much of this material is recognized as a vital part of the curriculum. Not, as may well be argued, as objectionable and oppressive texts to be contested or deconstructed in school, but as material which needs to be understood and integrated through reading and writing practices, with bridges being built to wider and different texts. Only by understanding the mythic quality of these fictions and by seeing both their pressing attraction and their oppressive potential, by seeing to the heart of the ways they 'work' with desire, can the literacy practices of school lay down other narratives, other possibilities, which are just as potent for the growing self and which help children to switch between them as they please.

Why do we care so much about the integration of the vast range of texts and messages that children read and receive? Is there not, as many educationalists argue, a case for having school literature tidily elevated and separated from what they consider to be the consumer-led productions of a vast and irresponsible factory of texts, many of which are cruel, violent and blatantly sexist? Having traced the potency of desire in many of these popular fictions, our answer lies in the notion of empowerment. The last link in the chain of argument is found in the subtle connection between consciousness and the growth of intellectual power. As Margaret Donaldson pointed out in her classic book *Children's Minds*:

> The point to grasp is how closely the growth of consciousness is related to the growth of the intellect. The two are not synonymous, for the growth of consciousness has much wider implications – but the link with intellectual growth is none the less intimate and profound. If the intellectual powers are to develop, the child must gain a measure of control over his own thinking and he cannot control it while he remains unaware of it. The attaining of this control means prising thought out of its primitive unconscious embeddedness in the immediacies of living in the world and reacting with other

human beings. It means learning to move beyond the bounds of human sense.[1]

If we consider that critical consciousness is developed by children looking inwards at their own mental processes, then it follows that by considering how certain texts yield pleasure, how they work on emotions and desires, and how in fact they are constructed, these readers have achieved a measure of control over their own thinking. Through immersing themselves in a rich variety of pleasurable texts, they are in a position to begin to develop critical consciousness. If, on the other hand, the texts they are working with are too unrelated to immediate experience and pleasure, too moral and removed, then young readers will fail to unlock them in meaningful ways. The literature of school, handed out by teachers who ignore pleasure becomes, as we have seen, framed by tediousness. We have seen in this book how popular texts, pulp fictions, videos are often the *familiar and pleasurable* ones, and it is here that the growth of the intellect must begin.

Throughout this book we have suggested and demonstrated how this immersion in pleasure and meaning must include the texts children currently read and watch outside school. This does not threaten the literacy curriculum, rather it enhances it, as children bring and reveal a shared context of meaning into the classroom. From this shared context a model of literacy learning is developed which relates, not to skills but to meanings. Once we begin to develop an attitude and a critical vocabulary to describe and evaluate popular texts, particularly media ones, to consider reality effects and emotional responses, to look behind the scenes at authorship and readership in the huge and profitable industry aimed at children, then we are in a position, not only to respect the sophisticated iconographic literacy that children are already using but also to present them with further texts, some of which will be books.

Throughout this book, too, we have seen evidence of children using a variety of texts and switching from iconography and the syntax of film to the business of reading and writing words. We have seen how young children, and adolescents, move between these different literacies, trying to make sense of one within the other. If, as this book argues, one area of their literacy is to be closed off from their school discourse, a whole area of experience is also truncated in a way that limits the growth of consciousness and ultimately the growth of the intellect. But the residual fear of many teachers is that the potency and pervasiveness of these popular and media fictions will crowd out the legitimate book culture of school. Then something of great value *to ourselves*, we feel, will be lost to our children and even greater losses exacted on the way we see and understand our intellectual culture. We fear that the genres and texts of our literate culture – the novel, the short story, the poem – with their great creative possibilities and enriching complexities will be closed to the children we teach. This offers us the challenge that we ourselves should perhaps begin to look inward and to examine our own fears. Where has our literate culture come from and how has it embedded itself in the many ways each of us make sense of our worlds? Did we not once and perhaps still luxuriate in less than intellectual pleasure? Are there not ways forward here for listening again to children and interpreting what they are telling us about textual pleasure and mapping it on to our own past fumbling experiences: the misconceptions, the secret readings of shameful texts, the rereadings of rubbish of our lost childish, and worse, adolescent selves? Does not intellectual growth start with desire?

THE BOOK CULTURE OF SCHOOL

Ironically it was a media text that first brought home to me how precious and yet how fragile was our culture of books: François Truffaut's now forgotten film of the 1960s, *Farenheit 451*. The title refers to the temperature at which books burn, and in the film they are cleared out by futuristically dressed firemen from homes and libraries, then torched. I cannot remember the plot, only a deadly determination by a state to rid its society of books, of book learning and book stories, to clean out every artefact of literate culture. A film which was inspired perhaps by similar activities of the young Chinese Red Guards in their cultural revolution. A sadness still affects me when I think of it because, like so many people, I have been changed, enriched, restored by books. Wet weekends, long journeys, times of rejection, of loneliness, of stasis, of exhaustion, of frustration, have all been transformed by reading.

Looking inwards at my own history of reading, examining my

own anxieties, being honest about my own history is perhaps a place to start. To me there is a feel, a smell, a tactile, human, take-it-or-leave-it friendliness to books which the high-technology worlds of film, television and computer communication cannot achieve. And the kinds of literacy that books assume in our culture I feel I can understand and manage. Some books are like old friends. They speak to me in wise and comforting ways and I know they bind me into a community of appreciative readers that stretches back to other generations. As a young Australian 12,000 miles away, brought up on English school stories, nineteenth-century novels and *Biggles'* books, I knew something of the inside, of the mental furniture of my adopted country long before I settled here. For me, as for many 'colonials', English literature had stretched long fingers into my consciousness and my sense of identity. And yet there are reasons for looking back on my reading pleasures with considerable embarrassment. I loved adventure stories of 'clean-limbed' Englishmen winning out against a variety of racial 'foes'. I gulped Enid Blyton, *Biggles*, Baroness Orczy, Georgette Heyer and *Nora of Billabong*. In fact, like most pre-television children, I read the most amazing quantity of 'rubbish'. Old magazines, comics and strange dusty novellas were raked for narrative pleasure. Although, like the children we teach, I read *actively*, laying down those literary texts alongside all the other meanings and messages my world revealed, I still feel they opened new possibilities, new philosophies, new subjective positions which I believe constantly helped me grow and act upon experience more thoughtfully, more consciously. Yet, looking back, none of them did I ever, really, totally *believe*. Each text provided a temporary universe of pleasure which I knew was false, yet I would not have been without it. My own feelings about the love and the power of such popular texts are, as for many teachers, where I can begin to understand children.

I have never met a teacher of literature who does not have a similar personal story of encounter and deep involvement with books. Behind the different chapters in this book runs a constant feeling for the power and potency of the written word. Yet perhaps we are out of date. Video, computer, television and interactive electronic books are pouring onto the market. Children are developing ways of reading that are highly iconographic, and these new texts and literacies seem to position them as readers in new postmodern postures. By this I mean that in these new texts meanings are not traditionally set out in the old familiar genres and narrative templates of folk tale and novel and, to a traditional reader, an increasing plethora of images seems linked to a lack of sustained and carefully unfolded meaning. Narrative ideas in the soaps appear to arrive, explode and fade like fireworks, new excitements replacing existing themes before they are 'properly' resolved. In other new texts the plot often becomes subsumed in a wealth of exciting contextual detail, leaving the text open, permeable and unending. New picture books for children are similarly open and challenging. Texts like *Aldo* and *Granpa* by John Burningham are not simply understated, they are wide open, cunningly inviting young readers to make narrative links and closures for themselves. Books by Anthony Browne are similarly multilayered, open, rich in suggestion and yet contain stories within stories, readings and textual possibilities which directly invite the activity and freedom of the reader to create his or her own meanings. Such picture books for children show breathtaking creative understanding of the rich possibilities of the new literacies.

Yet children, teenagers and adults still love *told* stories. The great narrative shapes provided in our culture by myth and folk tale, by the telling and performance by one firm and constant authorial voice, with one gaze of the teller and time moving constantly forward, stories with recognizable beginnings, middles and ends, are still there. In amongst a plethora of new and hybrid narrative forms, we can find evidence of narrative desire still working in its traditional form, the old told plot still providing a potent structure underlying many various and changing contextual details of our modern world. The arrest, the goose-pimples, the sudden intense quiet as a told story grips us in its ancient spell, striking into our imaginations with its familiar syntax, these emotions and responses are still with us, they still live in our children. Indeed, the culture industry knows this well. In addition to the familiar soaps and interactive postmodern fictions of television and computer, there is a steady production of what can only be described as 'traditional narrative'. Although made on film, the themes and structures of these narratives are the themes and structures of myth, of good against evil, of Romance quest, of chivalrous conduct, of true love. The good, the true, win out by constancy, courage and imagination against the forces of darkness and despair. The authorial position is held constant as we are invited to enjoy its all-powerful gaze. There are celebrations of triumphant masculinity through adventure and physical courage, and of triumphant femininity through beauty, innocence and honesty. And these fictions also connect our children, if we help them, to book culture.

So, through new forms of story *and* through understanding the workings of traditional narrative desire, we get children hooked on books. Through books *and* media texts, through the new and popular *and* the ancient and traditional, their worlds of cultural possibility are enlarged and enriched. They learn, ideally, to move from one text to the other with intellectual grace and ease. And if we continue to develop our model of literacy that cuts with consciousness, so too do we hand them the tools of *critical* consciousness. Through affective engagement with a multiplicity of texts they grow to read in multifarious ways: when, like us, they are tired with ragged psyches, they return to the bald narratives of desire, to simple adventures and romances; when they are fit and active they sharpen their wits on challenging complex stories, ones which contain more open possibilities, more diverse subject positions. Again, ideally, they move from one set of literacy practices to another, sometimes employing the new literacies critically and the old ones to satisfy desire; sometimes the other way round. The popular is thus valued, luxuriated in and interrogated in the same ways as literature. The long unproductive divorce between school literacy practices, with their improving and critical functions, and the often rough and ready texts and readings of desire from 'outside', with their uncritical intentions and soothing propensities, can, for the sake of our children, be mediated and bridged.

NOTE

1 Margaret Donaldson, *Children's Minds*, Glasgow: William Collins & Sons Ltd., 1978, p. 123.

Index